Enclosing the comn

Maynooth Studies in Local History

SERIES EDITOR   Raymond Gillespie

This volume is one of six short books published in the Maynooth Studies in Local History in 2004. Like their predecessors they are, in the main, drawn from theses presented for the M.A. course in local history at NUI Maynooth. Also, like their predecessors, they range widely over the local experience in the Irish past. That local experience is not simply the chronicling of events that happened within a narrow set of administrative or geographically-determined boundaries. Rather it encompasses all aspects of how the local communities of the past functioned from the cradle to the grave and from peer to peasant. The study of the local past is as much a reconstruction of mental worlds as of physical ones, where people agreed and disagreed over the way in which their world was to operate, and learned to live with consensus and division. The subject matter of these six short books includes the social context of marriage and of death in two very different settings and touches on many human activities between those rites of passage. Politics and dancing, both discussed in these books, may seem to be worlds that have little in common but at a local level both activities provided social gatherings at which people met and interacted, exchanged ideas, collaborated or disagreed, and made local societies work. In other cases disputes about how community assets such as common land are to be divided up can lay bare the often unspoken assumptions that local communities have about their world. Understanding such assumptions, which is best done on the spatially restricted level of the local community, remains the key to reconstructing how people in the past, at many levels from townland to nation, lived their lives. Such work is at the forefront of Irish historical scholarship and these short books, together with the earlier titles in the series, represent some of the most innovative and exciting work being done today not just in local studies but in Irish history as a whole. They also provide models which others can follow and adapt in their own studies of the reality of the Irish past. If they communicate something of the excitement of the vibrant world of Irish local history today then they will have done their work well.

Maynooth Studies in Local History: Number 57

Enclosing the commons

Dalkey, the Sugar Loaves and Bray, 1820–1870

Liam Clare

FOUR COURTS PRESS

Set in 10pt on 12pt Bembo by
Carrigboy Typesetting Services, County Cork for
FOUR COURTS PRESS LTD
7 Malpas Street, Dublin 8, Ireland
e-mail: info@four-courts-press.ie
http://www.four-courts-press.ie
and in North America for
FOUR COURTS PRESS
c/o ISBS, 920 N.E. 58th Avenue, Suite 300, Portland, OR 97213.

ISBN 1–85182–818–4

Printed in Ireland by
ßetaprint Ltd, Dublin

Contents

Acknowledgements		6
Introduction		7
1	The context of enclosure in Britain and Ireland	11
2	Dalkey: squatters sell on to speculators	29
3	The Sugar Loaves: seizures by squires spark off sedition	37
4	Bray: a structured solution	49
	Conclusion	58
	Notes	59

FIGURES

1	Location map – Dalkey commons	29
2	Dalkey village and commons, early 19th century – engraving	31
3	Location map – Kilmacanogue area	37
4	Old Long Hill/Ballinteskin Ridge	39
5	Location map – Bray commons	49
6	'On the commons of Bray' – [coloured] aquatint by Francis Jukes (1745–1812).	51

The cover incorporates *Lower Commons Bray, c.1820* by Williams Brocas (1794–1868).

Acknowledgements

I would like to thank the many people who helped with their advice, suggestions and searches, the staff of the National Archives, the National Library, the City Archives, the Gilbert Library and Wicklow County Libraries, especially Brian Donnelly, Aideen Ireland, Gregory O'Connor, Christy Allen, Tom Desmond, Mary Clark, Dr Máire Kennedy, Michael Kelleher and Robert Butler, as well as my fellow local historians, Brian White, John Callan, James Scannell and Redmond O'Hanlon. Máire Ní Chearbhaill deserves my special thanks for helping me to review my completed script. Most of all I thank Dr Raymond Gillespie, my editor, mentor and friend, for his many helpful suggestions and his guidance throughout this undertaking.

I wish to acknowledge with thanks Peter Pearson's agreement to my using the engraving of Dalkey,[1] and Mr John G. Doyle, Auctioneer, Bray for permission to reproduce the cover picture of the lower commons at Bray.[2]

Finally thanks to my wife, Carmel, for her patience and understanding in the course of this undertaking.

Introduction

This study explores the origin, evolution and decay of common land as a valuable community resource – both in Britain where the concept originated early, as part of the European-wide feudal system and in Ireland to which it was imported by the Anglo-Normans. The impact of the eventual, almost total, appropriation of commonage for exclusively individual use is examined in a variety of circumstances and through the contrasting experiences of three particular local communities which had enjoyed common land until the 19th century. These concern Dalkey, Co. Dublin, the Big and Little Sugar Loaf areas in north-east Co. Wicklow and Little Bray, now in Co. Wicklow but previously in Co. Dublin. The enclosing of common land has been progressing for more than a thousand years, and still continues. Its instigators were mainly landlords and larger tenants seeking to enhance their property by appropriating to themselves large areas of land previously available to the community. In addition, however, there were poverty-stricken squatters acting out of desperation, whose potato patches encroached along the edges of the commons. Also in the background were speculators who instinctively recognized an opportunity for profit. They all shared one trait, opportunism, by achieving enclosure either brazenly or surreptitiously as circumstances suggested. They often accomplished their objectives through the default of others.

Despite the previously pervasive presence of common lands throughout Ireland, little has been written about them, the most notable exception being J.H. Andrews' 'The struggle for Ireland's public commons'.[1] As will be seen below, although there are few original records remaining, the documents of the Quit Rent Office in the National Archives, and the published papers of various 19th-century royal commissions, especially those enquiring into municipal corporations, poverty and land issues, throw light on the subject. This material can be supplemented for local studies from local records.

The concept of commonage was unknown in Britain as long as there was a plentiful supply of land available to the small communities of hunters and farmers who roamed the primordial heaths and forests. But when the kings and nobles began to claim personal ownership of land, they encountered determined opposition from those who by custom and practice had enjoyed the freedom to use the countryside which was then being appropriated. The new landowners were constrained to recognize existing and ancient privileges, antecedent to the concept of private property, namely the rights of other people to use parts of the lands being appropriated. While the land had become privately owned, its use remained a common right, a right to take a profit out of lands belonging to someone else.[2] These common rights typically benefited all the inhabitants of a particular district, or a specific category of its inhabitants, rather than the public in general.

Typically, a manor settlement was set in an open countryside with few field boundaries. Each peasant had a 'close' or vegetable plot around his home. He was allocated a number of long, unfenced, scattered strips, each less than an acre in extent, for tillage in 'common fields'. The fenced-off meadow was also individually allocated, but once the hay had been saved, it became a seasonal common pasturage. Prior to harvest however, to protect both tillage and meadow from marauding animals, everyone's cattle, maintained as one herd, were moved away to rough pasturage or 'commons'. Finally, beyond all this lay the waste land or forest, which was only reclaimed for grazing or cultivating at a relatively late stage. The 'right of common', on the meadow in winter and on the commons and waste land throughout the year was the most valued possession of many peasants.[3]

There were different categories of commoners: 'landed commoners' entitled to shared pasturage and other rights, 'cottage commoners' with a right to graze a cow or two, or a few geese and landless commoners, 'living off the land rather than on it', furtively exercising limited, often ill-defined rights. The central communal right was the right of common pasturage. Lesser rights of a commoner could include estover (the right to gather firewood in forests), turbary (the right to cut turf) and piscary (the right to fish). As common rights evolved they became more complex: taking of wood from forests could be limited to timber for ploughs (plough bote), or for gates and fences (hedge bote), or for house repairs (house bote). In a subsistence and cashless economy, even small rights were of importance, like harvesting bracken for fuel or as cattle-bedding, or over-wintering of cattle on meadows (shack), or grazing sheep in summer (sheep-walk), or a lord's right to require tenants to fold their sheep on his demesne lands for manuring purposes (foldage). At a later period other rights less linked to basic subsistence were developed, such as fowling, warren (breeding of rabbits), quarrying, mining and so on.[4] Most significantly, the rights in a particular manor or feudal lordship sought to meet the tenants' needs for food and clothing and for housing and heat, by the fullest utilisation of local resources. Moreover, these rights were only part of a much wider mesh of responsibilities and rights which gave a social framework and a stability to the community.[5] While initially the common land was freely accessible only to commoners of a particular manor, the general public in many cases secured rights by adverse possession over an extended period of time. In the long term, the erosion of the commons reflected the wider trend from a social system based on community rights to a milieu in which the rights of the individual began to take precedence over the common good. From the late 16th century, lessees began to secure rights like common pasture or turbary only for the periods of their leases. Such commons were private commons; public commons were not terminable on the expiry of leases.[6]

Common lands were found in every locality and included in particular, upland pasture, woodland and forests and marshy areas which dried out in summer. They were never, as noted above, 'no-man's land'; ownership of commons was held by the lord of the manor, or by default in later centuries, by the crown. The proverbial 'village green', a late addition to common land, was the most typical of lowland commons. Rights still exist on some of England's 1,354 village greens for the grazing of geese, and for participation in recreational activities. Traditionally commons were used for festivals, holiday activities, fresh air and recreation. A great number of English towns developed from casual assemblies of traders on the periphery of common land, on places such as waste ground beside a river ford or near a cross roads. Liverpool is probably the best known of these towns but there were very many others. The names of many surviving English commons are well-known in Ireland: Broadmoor, Dartmoor, Exmoor, Sherwood Forest in the country-side, and in London, Wimbledon Common, Clapham Common, Hampstead Heath, Blackheath, Tooting Bec and Epping Forest. The public enjoyment of the remaining commons in Britain is underwritten by statute; there is no parallel legislation in Ireland.[7]

The invading Anglo-Normans rapidly established their familiar legal and administrative systems in Ireland, particularly in the south-eastern areas. In their English-style manors, populated by English settlers, an open-field system of agriculture was established, with typical scattered strips of individually-held, cultivable land, supplemented by grazing on common pastures, turf from the bogs, timber from the forest and other benefits of the system of commonage.[8] Not all 'commonage' in Ireland, however, had its origin in the manorial system. In early Irish law, there was a parallel indigenous recognition of both common and private rights on uncultivated land, which was apparently vested in the túath. In more modern times, particularly in the west and north, the openfield 'rundale system' emerged, typically featuring potato gardens, permanently cultivated infields, periodically cultivated pastoral outfields and additional summer transhumance or 'booley' pastures. Such lands were collectively farmed by extended families holding joint tenancies. 'Booleying' on its own was an ancient custom but whether the entire rundale system is pre-Anglo-Norman or a 17th-century development is still being argued. But it is certain that when an increasing population began to colonize new outlying districts, new 'commonage' was created from waste lands.[9]

Elsewhere, while many borough corporations date from the Anglo-Norman invasion, the establishment of later borough commons can be found in the surviving 'template' used for the charters of 17th-century plantation towns established by James I. The promoters of these towns were typically given grants of land to support their economy and for town facilities such as church, school-house, playground and a town common 'for meadow, pasture, and turbarie' for the benefit of 'all inhabitants and townsmen' as at Lifford, Co. Donegal or 'for the only benefit of those which had not town acres for corn or grass' as at Killyleagh.[10] J.H. Andrews categorizes public commons as: territorial commons, where the rights belonged to the inhabitants of a territory; royal commons which was crown land; manorial commons (mainly in the Anglo-Norman areas) where the lord of the manor owned the land but the rights to use it belonged to its inhabitants; borough commons owned by a borough corporation, and jointly-owned commons where adjoining owners failed to define a common boundary within, for example, impenetrable bogland.[11]

1. The context of enclosure in Britain and Ireland

BRITAIN

The clear distinction between the physical erection of fences and the extinguishing of common rights reflects two distinct common meanings for the word 'enclosure'. The first meaning describes the change in the landscape, from open, unfenced 'fields', to today's hedged-in smaller units. Such enclosure did not necessarily involve privatizing the common lands; its main purpose was to check the movement of livestock. The second meaning of enclosure, used here, is the appropriation of all or parts of the commons, either in large tracts or as small cottage plots for individual use.[1] The word 'inclosure' was the statutory and legal form, both versions stemming from the Latin *inclaudere*. 'Encroachment' was the term commonly used for the taking-over of cottage or larger plots where the occupier had no legal authority to do so. The essential difference therefore between 'enclosure' and 'encroachment' was that of legal sanction.

The designation and subsequent enclosure of common lands are each part of the same movement; they do not represent conflicting processes. There was no clear-cut point in time when the creation of commons was complete. Moreover, creation and enclosure of commonage overlapped over an extended period of time. The concept of commonage had only gradually been established as a forced, uneasy stalemate rather than a final settlement. The very same pressure from the powerful nobles to appropriate property was to continue beyond the compromise of commonage, until they had virtually completed the process of converting the landmass of Britain from a resource available to all, into a privately-owned form of wealth. Both the recognition of commons and their subsequent enclosure moved forward over the centuries at varying rates according to the diverse conditions of time and place.

As early as the 13th century, even though widespread enclosure was still centuries into the future, the pressures were beginning to show. The powerful magnates and landowners were inhibited from profiting from their 'wastes, woods and pastures' due to their tenants' rights of common pasture thereon. The Statute of Merton passed in 1235 in response to their complaints, authorized them to appropriate waste land provided that sufficient (common) pasture remained to satisfy the needs of the tenants.[2] Constitutionally, the Statute of Merton was a landmark, being the first act of parliament in the printed *Statutes of the Realm* in Britain; it was eventually repealed in Britain in 1948 and in Ireland by the Statute Law Revision Act, 1983. After Merton, the lords increased their pressure on the powers and privileges of the peasants.

Nevertheless, enclosure of commons remained relatively insignificant for as long as the economic and social pressures of population growth, the level of agricultural production, the nation's relative wealth and social structures remained stable and in equilibrium. However, by the second half of the 16th century, further signs of pressure on the system were emerging. There was the widespread 'stinting' or rationing of common pasture, to avoid over-grazing by limiting the number of animals to be pastured and apportioning the limit between commoners. There was also the encroachment by landless squatters on waste land. Eventually the pressures to enclose became unstoppable.[3]

This enclosure of commons was achievable in several ways: by process of law (buying out of commoners' rights); by withdrawal of 'common by sufferance' (ending of previously-condoned illegal use of commons); by approvement (where enclosure left a reasonable remainder for the commoners);[4] by agreement (sometimes a euphemism for disagreement, where only extreme pressure secured the commoners' agreement), or by statutory enclosure through acts of parliament.[5] Rights could also be lost through disuse over time or by unchallenged possession.

In Britain, from the mid-18th century, an extensive political movement pleading the noblest of motives and the national interest, emerged to promote enclosure as a means of securing greater efficiency in agriculture.[6] Most contemporary arguments were one-sided, however, advancing the interests of the predominant land-owning class, though there were some articulate and vigorous middle-class champions putting forward the views of the peasants. Resulting from enclosure, the removal of the income and status inherent in common rights eliminated the long-established rural English communal social structure and turned the nation's independent peasantry into an unskilled working class, utterly dependent on others for employment and entirely bereft of economic security.[7] While many historians today emphasize the social consequences of enclosure, in reaction to the earlier predominant economic and agricultural arguments, the economic benefits to the English people as a whole should not be overlooked: unused or under-utilized lands were indeed brought into use; lands were drained; roads were built; a larger population could be fed; labour was freed to produce the industrialization of Britain.[8]

Two of the *dramatis personae* in the political arena of the British enclosure debate had Irish connections. Arthur Young, the greatest of English writers on agriculture, lived off-and-on for some years in Mitchelstown, Co. Cork, and is best known here for accounts of his Irish travels in 1776–9. He was principled in his promotion of the philosophy of maximizing the net product of agriculture, and was intemperate in his crusade for enclosure. He showed antipathy to absentee landlords, to antiquated cultivation methods, to wastes and commons and to small holdings. Yet he was not without compassion for the poor, describing the Irish landlords' middlemen as, inter alia, 'the most oppressive species of tyrant ...', 'bloodsuckers of the poor tenantry'. Moreover, he saw the cultivation of waste lands and the provision of new cow-pastures as the means of relieving pauperism rather than the cause of it.[9] William Cobbett, author, journalist and radical, unlike Young, was of peasant stock and had personal experience of the misery produced by enclosing the countryside. He was among the minority who vociferously opposed its social effects. Cobbett viewed Irish political objectives as inseparable from the struggles of English working people, fearing that any dominance of Irish landlords over their tenantry would spread to landlords and industrialists in Britain.[10] He occasionally stayed with his friend, General Sir George Cockburn at Shanganagh Castle, Shankill, Co. Dublin. Sir George, as will be seen later, supported the ordinary people in both the enclosure of Dalkey Commons in 1824 and the Loughlinstown incident of 1847.

Much enclosure of commons in Britain was effected by private statute in circumstances where agreement to enclose could not be achieved among the proprietors of a parish or township. Such legislation conformed to two stated principles: first, that enclosed land should be shared proportionately by those with a legal interest in the common, and secondly, that a small minority, based on acreage rather than the number of persons involved, should not frustrate a proposed enclosure. The first Inclosure act was passed in 1709. The final number of English Inclosure acts passed, depends on the definition of the term, but one estimate suggests slightly fewer than 5,000. A General Inclosure act was passed in 1845, and statutory enclosure in general came to an end in 1869.[11] Each act delegated powers to named commissioners and surveyors. Between them they surveyed the commons, considered claims to rights of commonage and made awards. They laid out roads and rights-of-way, arranged for public works and levied finance to cover expenses. While the legislative principles may have appeared to be fair and necessary to meet the need for greater agricultural output and the feeding of a rapidly increasing population, there was hardship for, and dissent by, many of the peasants, who lost the foundation of their economic and social stability. Many peasants could not prove a legal claim to rights on the common. Others could not afford to fence and drain any allotment they would receive. Some successful claimants, soon sold their allocated land to speculators and moved away, being joined by other successful claimants who had been paid off in cash.[12] The multiplicity of parliamentary acts reflects the substantial dissention among the propertied classes who endorsed enclosure in principle but required adjudication on their conflicting claims in the resulting redistribution.[13]

Partly through the activities of the Commons Preservation Society founded in 1865, the process of enclosure was checked. The Metropolitan

Commons act of 1866 ended the inclosure of any commons within the Metropolitan Police District of London. Ten years later, the Commons act of 1876 severely limited the rights to enclose anywhere in Britain. In particular, private rights to enclose by 'approvement' was restricted. Today even the local authorities' powers to acquire lands compulsorily for public use are severely constrained where common land is involved.[14]

The 'pastoral poet' and agricultural labourer, ploughboy and lime-burner, John Clare, was a native of Helpston in Cambridgeshire, a parish which was enclosed between 1809 and 1820, making Clare an angry man. He is the pre-eminent source for the peasants' view of enclosure:

> These paths are stopt – the rude philistines thrall
> Is laid upon them and destroyed them all
> Each little tyrant with his little sign
> Shows where man claims earth glows no more divine
> But paths to freedom and to childhood dear
> A board sticks up to notice 'no road here'
> And on the tree with ivy overhung
> The hated sign by vulgar taste is hung.[15]

Clare, unstable, uneducated and unscientific, gave an emotional rather than a detached analysis of the local upheavals, but his poetry and prose presents through the medium of local colour and dialect, a unique response to the social, rather than the economic, results of enclosure. He wrote from the perspective of one who has seen the destruction of the social milieu of his youth 'that made as equals, not as slaves, the poor', and reminds us that as well as economic trauma, there was intangible impoverishment for the landless labourers.[16] Oliver Goldsmith wrote on the same theme some 50 years earlier. He claimed that his 'Deserted Village', written in London in 1770, was factually based on his travels, though he feared that his readers would consider it to be a product of his imagination.[17]

IRELAND

As in Britain, the process of enclosure in Ireland probably commenced in a piecemeal fashion immediately after the manorial system was established here in the early 13th century, with tenants grasping any opportunity to enhance their own possessions by exchanging and consolidating their cultivated strips, or by colonising peripheral lands. But these were relatively minor incursions; widespread enclosure came much later.[18] The continuing prevalence of common land in the mid-17th century is evidenced by the many, though not comprehensive, references to commons in the Civil Survey of 1654 to 1656. Moreover, the surveyors for the contemporary Down

Survey were specifically instructed to record details of commonage, an instruction which was not always carried out.[19] Existing town commons were typically renewed in the new borough charters of that period.[20]

The agricultural reorganization of the late 18th and early 19th century produced a strong economic rationale for the enclosure of commons. 'Agricultural improvement' based on scientific techniques and commercialization, together with the increased rural population, and general economic trends from 1780 to 1820, favoured tillage as against livestock production. These trends, together with the decay of the old manorial system, encouraged appropriation of the commons both by landlords' enclosure schemes and by settlements of landless squatters. The landowners' enclosure schemes created regular fields; the squatters' encroachments resulted in uncoordinated, disorderly settlements and left behind most irregularly-shaped commons.[21] During this period, most remaining areas of woodland and scrub were cleared and the old commons previously used for rough grazing were transformed by liming and draining.[22] However, not all the enclosed common lands were semi-waste; while they included mainly upland pasture, marshy areas, forests and waste lands, they often also included good arable land. An essential difference between the British and Irish experience, was that the displaced labourer in Britain had the outlet of moving to rapidly-growing urban areas fed by the industrial revolution, whereas in Ireland the dispossessed sought alternative shelter on nearby estates or a commons, while competing for whatever labouring employment was available locally, or 'travelling', that is, going begging. Many emigrated if financially possible.[23]

Arthur Young described in detail the state of Irish agricultural development at the end of the 18th century and noted the enclosure of waste lands which was then proceeding apace. He considered the enclosure of waste ground to be easier in Ireland than in England because the rights of commonage, 'the curse of our moors', 'have no existence in Ireland'. This was not in fact true and Young himself noted that the common people kept sheep on the mountains. During his period of residence in Co. Cork, he wrote:

> His lordship by my advice, encouraged the peasantry to take in small parts of these mountains themselves. The adjoining farms being out of lease, he had a power of doing what he pleased; I marked a road, and assigned a portion of waste on each side to such as were willing to form the fences in the manner prescribed, to cultivate and inhabit the land, allowing each a guinea towards his cabin and promising the best land rent free for three years.[24]

While there may have been no formal rights of common in Young's area of north Co. Cork, there were still unenclosed commonages elsewhere. The privatizing of land, which had been understood by the population to be commonage was one of the factors leading to agrarian protest by the Whiteboys and others after 1760; nevertheless, the violent opposition was fairly limited.[25]

In the early 19th century, particularly outside Leinster, intense population pressures reinforced by landlord avarice, pushed the peasantry to reclaim and colonize what had previously been waste lands.[26] In the process, the old rundale system of collective farming on a common tenancy was at first extended but later collapsed through over-subdivision, at which stage dispersed farms replaced the former communal settlements and organization.[27] Enclosure was nearly complete in most areas before 1870, but the process still dragged on, particularly in some mountainous areas, boosted for example, by the need to stop different flocks of sheep mixing as a disease-prevention measure.

Not all commons consisted of large tracts of land. There were numerous areas of roadside ground which neither formed parts of the highway nor of the adjoining land. They were part of the manorial waste and belonged to the lord of the manor.[28] They too became the targets of both enclosing landlords and encroaching squatters. John Bush, a visitor to Ireland described the situation in 1764:

> There are many little commons, or vacant spots of ground, adjacent to the road, upon which the inhabitants of the cabins by the high-wayside have been used, from time immemorial, to rear, as they express it, a pig or goose, which they have bought very young, the sale of which has helped to furnish them with a few necessaries. Many of these have been taken into fields or enclosures on the roadside by the landlords, who have farmed or purchased them, or the lords of the manor. From an impartial view of their situation, I could not from my soul, blame these unhappy delinquents. They are attacked and reduced on all sides, so hardly, as to have barely their potatoes left them to subsist on.[29]

Arthur Young also gave a vivid description of roadside squatters:

> There are a great many cabins, usually by the roadside, or in the ditch, which have no potato gardens at all … A wandering family will fix themselves under a dry bank, and with a few sticks, furze, fern, etc., make up a hovel much worse than an English pigsty, support themselves how they can, by work, begging and stealing; if the neighbourhood wants hands, or takes no notice of them, the hovel grows into a cabin … I have passed places in the road one day without any appearances of a habitation, and next morning found a hovel, filled with a man and woman, six or eight children, and a pig.[30]

The demise of borough commons is relatively well documented. These were lost to their original purpose in such a variety of ways that they can be considered a microcosm of enclosure generally. The loss of these commons, however, cannot be considered in isolation from the almost universal alienation of the towns' other corporate lands. An extensive catalogue of misappropriation exists in the records of the royal commission which examined the municipal boroughs in the 1830s: 'alienated blatantly', 'no scruples', 'no sense of trust', 'sold … to some of themselves for little or nothing', 'rent … sunk into private pockets', 'property … lost through usurpation and neglect', 'misconduct and mismanagement', 'they deprived themselves of … being useful'. In many cases, the land originally granted for the benefit of the inhabitants went to the civic leaders in their private, rather than their corporate capacities. Moreover, the corporations soon became closed shops with the commonality or inhabitants being excluded from the self-perpetuating, ever-decreasing inner circle of freemen holding onto power, privilege and property. This eventually resulted in the land, including the commons which had been provided for the welfare of the inhabitants generally, becoming the personal property of freemen's descendents or of purchasers from the freemen.[31]

Whether misappropriated by civic officials or not, many commons were fenced in and sold off, or were let to individuals. Borough commons like those at Naas, Portarlington, Carrickfergus, Enniskillen, Killybegs, Lifford, Cashel and others were enclosed by their owners, whether these were the corporations themselves or purchasers from the corporations. They were sometimes enclosed subject to buying off other claimants, as at Maryborough and Ardee and perhaps Dundalk. Those at Dingle and Navan were enclosed by tenants with the connivance of their landlords to whom the land would 'revert' when the tenants' leases expired. They were enclosed by tenants at Banagher and by a sole tenant at Kildare when the corporation stopped collecting rent. They were acquired by the limited body of burgesses and freemen 'leasing for life' at Trim, by the lord of the soil and his tenants in a formal partitioning at Lifford, and by the landlord and his neighbours at Philipstown. Even this list does not exhaust the various potential scenarios for enclosure; no two local experiences were exactly the same.[32]

Not all enclosure represented misappropriation. In Bangor, the inhabitants willingly gave up their rights to enable their lands to be let, with the income going for the purchase of spinning wheels or looms for the poor or some similar charitable purpose. After Drogheda enclosed its commons, the ground was leased in lots by public cant or auction, the rents going to charitable purposes. Belturbet corporation made some charitable grants of cottage sites on the common, although Catholics were excluded. A site on 'The Irish Street Commons' in Armagh was allocated for a charity vocational school.[33]

Encroachment on the borough commons occurred opportunistically when control by the owners was abandoned for any reason: at Ardfert and Duleek when their controlling corporations became defunct, at Swords, Fethard and Navan when the portreeve gave up intervening, at Kildare when the corporation lost a court case and at Carrickfergus, Kilmallock and Dingle when the corporation took no action against it. While encroachment was the extreme consequence of absence of control, less dramatic symptoms also appeared: free-for-all grazing on the commons at Kildare, Carrickfergus, Duleek and Swords and 'skinning' of the surface for fuel at Carrickfergus. Conversely, squatters were successfully resisted at Bangor. Encroachment could occur over an extended period as at Carlingford or within a few years as at Swords.[34]

Some commons still survived to the time of the municipal corporations enquiry of the early 1830s. Belturbet corporation was issuing tickets to permit grazing on the commons under a scheme based on property held – though Catholics were not allocated tickets. However, over-grazing was occurring and cattle had to be removed on alternate months. Some locals argued that the commons should be leased permanently to produce income for the public good. In Kells the civic officials and freemen got four-year leases of lots to be farmed within a framework of rotation of crops among six fields, but in the early 1830s, a large extent of Kells' common was taken possession of by some 500 to 600 persons. The Murrough in Wicklow town also remained a common with grazing rationed by 'stinting' to one horse or cow per freeman. Commoners still exercised their rights at Carlingford on those parts of the poorer lands which remained open.[35]

While custom and practice required that commons be left undeveloped, such lands were frequently utilized for public events, works and buildings, especially in urban areas. Troops were mustered, criminals executed and civic gatherings held there, on what was often the most convenient open space. Schools were erected on commons and in later times, railways and work-houses.[36] Roads often hugged the inside of a commons boundary presumably for reasons of cost, examples being the section of the main Dublin to Wicklow road at Sunnybank, Bray, and the Kilmacanogue to Roundwood road around the Sugar Loaf.[37] The quarrying of materials free of charge from nearby commons for road building and maintenance was also permitted by legislation.[38]

In Ireland, there was nothing similar to the British parliamentary enclosure movement. An 18th-century statutory framework delegated to local courts and commissioners the detail of local enclosures.[39] The Irish parliament, apart from enclosures in special situations, such as Ballybough and Merrion Square,[40] only passed its first individual enclosure act (for Dromiskin commons, Co. Louth) months before the Union in 1800.[41] Hervey, Viscount Mountmorres, in a pamphlet published in 1796, suggested to English politicians the administrative advantages of the system of Irish enclosure legislation,[42] under which general acts delegated power to courts and commissions, and individual enclosure acts were unknown, in contrast to the 1,600 individual acts in Britain. Reactions in England to his suggestions referred to the different circumstances between Ireland and England, most notably the smaller number of 'tracts of waste lands with commons and mixed rights and properties' in Ireland.[43] Some Irish general enclosure acts were specifically aimed at reclaiming waste – unproductive – land while others dealt specifically with lands held jointly or in common, so it is necessary to restate that waste areas were not all held in common and not all common lands were 'waste'.

Arguably the earliest Irish enclosure act was passed in 1542,[44] although the Statute of Merton (1235) had been applied to Ireland through Poynings' act of 1495.[45] The 1542 act authorized the court of chancery to decide on an application by a joint tenant or tenant-in-common to have a joint holding partitioned. Over a century later, in 1697, a temporary act, made permanent in 1707, was passed to facilitate and expedite the partitioning of jointly-held or common land.[46] Within the next generation, the three basic Irish enclosure acts were passed, in 1715, 1721 and 1731 respectively, permitting the partitioning of waste or unfenced lands within the framework of the judicial process. The 1715 act was passed 'to encourage the draining and improvement of bogs and unprofitable grounds' which were useless to the owners, impassable and inaccessible, a hindrance to inland commerce, a harbour for malefactors, and 'an occasion of corrupt air'. It envisaged the improving of communications, particularly waterways, draining and improving access, giving employment to the poor and increasing the public revenues. Commissioners were to implement the act, their power being balanced by local commissioners to determine disputes through mediation and arbitration.[47] The 1721 act was passed 'to oblige proprietors and tenants of neighbouring grounds to make fences between their several lands and holdings', subject to court approval of a petition by any one proprietor, tenant or occupier.[48] The third general act, passed in 1731, was introduced and pushed through by Arthur Dobbs, member of parliament for Carrickfergus, an agricultural polemicist.[49] It was entitled 'an act to encourage the improvement of barren and waste land and bog and for planting of timber trees and orchards'. Under this act any person possessed of land adjoining a bog, moss, lough or tidal lands could lodge a petition in court for the ascertaining of bounds. The court could establish a commission to examine witnesses, and a jury to determine existing bounds or create new ones. The commission could drain the area and apportion the costs subject to court approval.[50] In summary, the first act established the organizational framework for enclosing of large waste areas; the second facilitated the partitioning of unfenced land; the third provided for creating new boundaries and enclosing of waste ground.

While these statutes existed, and although no contemporary commentator is recorded as contradicting Mountmorres' eulogizing of the situation, there is little evidence of the legislation having been widely used. On the contrary, in 1813 a royal enquiry reported a huge extent of unreclaimed bog due, it argued, to stalemate whenever tenants with arable land around the edges claimed a right to turn their cattle onto the bog, and had tenures insufficient for investing in reclamation themselves, though more than sufficient to render reclamation impracticable for the landlord through fear of litigation. 'Legislative intervention' was recommended to facilitate determination of new boundaries and compensation for rights. Similar evidence was given to a further enquiry some 13 years later, arguing that a landlord of waste land going to court had a certainty of nothing but expense. Again, further evidence to another investigation claimed that a writ of partition from the court of chancery, besides being expensive was frequently 'on account of some technicality' impossible to get.[51] In 1805, an 'Irish commonable lands bill' was submitted to the British house of lords for partitioning the remaining common lands of Ireland, implying that there was dissatisfaction with existing legislation. This bill was rejected, however. The lord chancellor opined that the proposers considered it as easy to divide up a commons as an estate within a family.[52] So Mountmorres' claim as to the efficacy of Irish legislation appears to have been, at least, exaggerated.

If Irish enclosure legislation was so defective, how did the commons become enclosed? There were many reasons. We could state almost as a principle that commons could continue in existence only as long as there was a stability based on an equilibrium of power between the landowners, the tenants-in-common and the general populace. Consequently if for more than a few years any one of the interests secured a dominance whereby they could impose their will, by law, by intimidation or by pay-off, the commons was at risk of being privatized. Moreover, enclosure or encroachment once achieved, was virtually irreversible. In Ireland, unlike Britain, the elimination of rights of commonage was greatly facilitated, during and after the 17th-century confiscations and re-granting of property, by the totality of disruption caused by the substitution of new lords on new estates, new tenants on new holdings and new conditions in new tenures.[53] Again, the newly arrived English land-owners were more investors than farmers, were well aware of current English trends towards enclosure and had little loyalty to Irish custom and practice. Even the borough corporations, far from preserving their towns' rights of commonage for the benefit of their citizens, almost universally put private interests before public responsibility and alienated the great bulk of their common land for individual use. Legally, the centuries-old tradition of common rights on manorial lands became irrelevant wherever lands were confiscated and re-granted by the crown without maintaining the continuity of their earlier rights. Alternatively where common rights had not been declared forfeit, the lands were still at risk; a new grantee would have no legal responsibility for them even though the lord of the manor would no longer be on the scene.[54] Because of the new trend towards the issuing of leases for limited terms, forceful landowners could negotiate away any traditional rights on renewal without having to resort to the courts or to legislation. Such solutions would only be used where agreements or intimidation didn't work. Absence of documentation also hindered the preservation of commons. Most manor courts had kept few records to prove the existence of commons; the Civil or Down surveys did not record them comprehensively. Deeds protecting rights were prepared only between near-equals, to avoid litigation; many tenancies between people of different status were verbal or at will. Landlords often connived at the enclosure of commons by their tenants, knowing that the lands enclosed would revert to them at the end of the tenant's lease.[55] The great bulk of people, differing in race, language and religion from the new aristocracy, facing the overwhelming power of the administration and remaining voiceless in the courts of law where they couldn't afford to litigate, had little legal opportunity to protect their rights, if change was imposed from above. They were also so impoverished as to be unable to resist if even minimal offers of cash, or a low-rent short-term tenancy or a re-location were offered. They sometimes triumphed, however, when large numbers were ready to threaten violence, as described later, or when a landlord did not pursue his case.

Less than a dozen enclosure acts relating to individual commons in Ireland were passed at Westminster between the act of Union and Irish independence, the last being in 1862. Later, the Land Commission, and subsequently the Minister for Agriculture, Food and Rural Development, got powers under the land acts compulsorily to partition commonages. These powers are now subject to planning legislation and EC environmental impact regulations.[56]

The case of Coolquoy commons at Kilsallaghan in north Co. Dublin demonstrates how the legal process of enclosure during the 19th century could lean heavily on an individual. Eight years prior to this enclosure in 1827, David Shanley, a poor labourer, was dislodged by enclosure from another part of the same commons, and moved to a site of under two acres just north of the present Coolquoy Lodge on the Ashbourne Road. Here he built a thatched cabin for his family and planted potatoes and oats. When Coolquay was being legally enclosed, no lord of the manor could be found, so the crown as 'lord paramount of the soil of the entire kingdom' was allocated a portion – the very triangle which Shanley and two other plot-holders occupied. The crown estate officials were not even aware of their allocation until 1831 when possession was to be taken and the ejectment of Shanley and the others was initiated. While legally not entitled to remain by 'squatters' rights', Shanley would be paid £1 16s. 8½d. compensation for his limited interest in the property – based on its agricultural value but disregarding its valuable situation on a main road. Shanley, through a literate acquaintance, wrote to the crown estates 'without wish or desire to give his majesty any trouble', claiming 20 years' presence on the common, stating that he could not afford to buy the property but offering to lease it at prevailing local rates. He had nowhere to go. Eighteen months later the site was sold at public auction. There is no record of what happened to Shanley.[57]

Securing an enclosure act did not always mean success for the proprietors promoting the legislation. No doubt obstinate squatters often had to be 'bought off', as will be seen below at Bray commons. However, exceptional obstacles were encountered while implementing the Ballymore Eustace Enclosure act of 1814. The various commons close to the town were of good quality and shared for grazing. One 'fine large common' was described in 1788 as 'a very agreeable sight to see, so many cattle of different sorts pleasingly feeding on the sweet grass, as rich as any meadow produces'.[58] In 1816, the nominated surveyors were driven off the commons by the occupants 'who had resided there from time immemorial' in cabins with gardens and with cattle pastured on the common. Reacting to the proposed enclosure, the inhabitants partitioned the commons among themselves and had it enclosed, divided and tilled. Then, reinforced by a much greater number of new occupiers, they expressed their determination to resist any further survey by force. A local magistrate was recruited by the enclosure commissioners and he sought support of infantry and cavalry to preserve the peace when a new attempt at surveying was to be made in July 1819. It took a year to secure the military aid and when the surveyors eventually arrived back on site in July 1820, supported by 20 cavalry and 17 infantry, the inhabitants resisted in such great numbers and were so violent in their opposition, that there was little possibility of the survey being carried out without bloodshed. The survey was called off. A further survey (essential for implementing the act) was planned for 4.00 a.m. one morning that autumn, with sufficient troops 'to intimidate the public, and thereby avoid violence'. The military did not respond; they feared that 'some poor people would be killed'. A reminder was sent to Dublin Castle exactly a year later; the file was closed after an unminuted interview between the military and one of the enclosure commissioners.[59] By 1851 over 100 families held freehold plots on the commons. Some were within the town; others dispersed around the Broadleas commons, 465 statute acres in extent.[60] The example of Ballymore Eustace had a knock-on effect at nearby Kilcullen where, following an abortive petition from a local priest to have the commons drained some 800 people, 'peasant vagrants', took over the commons despite having had their ditches levelled twice, and erected their cabins there.[61]

Not all squatted-on commons were so extensive as at Ballymore Eustace or Kilcullen. By 1851 Rathnew commons, Co. Wicklow, just over six acres in extent, had been occupied by some 660 persons living in 156 houses. In 1770, the proprietor of the commons, a Miss Blake of Rathdrum, had let it be known that she would not disturb squatters there. In the early 1840s 'a comfortable class of labourers' evicted from eight or ten cottages by the agent on the Carroll estate at Ashford had found refuge at Rathnew.[62] This may have helped it to increase its population by 8.5 per cent during the famine decade.[63] Nationally there were hundreds of encroachments ranging from the large, organized take-overs of common land to the individual homeless family lying low on a tiny, secluded, derelict site.

Contemporaneously with the 18th-century enclosure-facilitating legis-lation, other statutes were enacted to 'protect' commons against 'waste', that is, encroachment mainly by the homeless. An act in 1789, 29 Geo III c.30, authorized the imposing of jail sentences for 'skinning the commons' (taking the surface for fuel), and the impounding of pigs found rooting (grazing) there without ringed snouts.[64] This act was amended in 1791, so that county grand juries on receipt of a sworn complaint could seek a judge's authority to abate any encroachments such as enclosing a part of the commons, or building 'any house, hut or cabbin' thereon.[65] Appointment of commons inspectors was authorized in 1796, with only limited success, as only commons exceeding 2,000 acres were covered.[66] A special power was given in the 1791 act to inhibit encroachment on the Curragh by building an eight-foot road along its boundary. The 'Curragh' meaning a racecourse, previously called 'Saint Brigid's pastures', has been recorded from early historical times as a pasture. It survives as a commons for sheep under the Curragh act of 1870.[67]

The anti-encroachment legislation was ineffective, judging by the immediate need for two amending acts, an apparent unwillingness even then to use the legislation and a rapid expansion of squatting. Nevertheless, these acts were invoked by some land-owners, for example in Loughlinstown, Co. Dublin, in 1847. The larger section of Loughlinstown Commons, between what are now Saint Columcille's hospital and the Silver Tassie public house, had already been settled by squatters. It still displays the tell-tale disorderly layout. Francis Carter, a resident living close to Shanganagh Bridge, took exception to the existence of a tiny squatters' hut some six feet square, erected on a corner of the commons at its eastern end, a few metres from his front entrance. The hut was occupied by two washerwomen named Kavanagh with their mother. He brought them before the magistrates under the primary act against encroachment, known as '29th Geo III' and they were fined £5 or two months imprisonment, though the matter was then left in abeyance. Carter then approached the grand jury charging the house as a nuisance, but the jury refused to present the charge at a higher court, and dismissed the decision of the magistrates. There is no surviving record of how he succeeded in getting the women sent to jail, but an immediate appeal was made on their behalf. Unluckily for Carter the case was heard by Judge Crampton who had a few years previously ruled that encroachment was not a crime in itself but only became an offence after the quasi-judicial presentment of the situation as a nuisance by the grand jury. The women were released, and when word reached the locality, a reported 2,000 people assembled on the common, with over 100 cars and horses, some bringing stone, others sand for mortar, yet others slates or timber, and within a day and a half a slated house had been constructed and furnished to replace their hut. During the construction work, some employees of Mr Carter arrived and attempted to intervene. The police were summoned from Bray. A magistrate read the riot act and rode away, leaving the police at the scene to handle any subsequent riot. Some hours later when Carter's men tried to interfere with the work, the police intervened and complaints were made against the aggressors. One of the men charged was sent for trial. General Sir George Cockburn, a magistrate, said that rather than being a nuisance, the house was a very great improvement to the common.[68]

Unrelated to encroachment, some legal regulation of surviving commons was essential where a stand-off between the various parties pre-empted any management control. Typically in such circumstances, there were complaints and squabbling over the hogging of the more productive areas, the numbers of cattle grazed, the driving away of rivals' cattle, the dumping of refuse, the setting of fires, the 'skinning' of the surface for fuel, and the presence of gypsies and nomads. Indeed the presence of gypsies was often a convenient excuse for enclosure.[69]

The legislators who passed the anti-encroachment legislation failed to recognize the misery and social injustice represented by squatting on commons, characterising encroachments as 'receptacles of idle and disorderly persons'. A royal commission on municipal corporations in the 1830s heard one site referred to as 'a place affording settlement to persons of bad character'. A surveyor for the Ordnance Survey described one location as 'a great number of mud cabins inhabited by the lowest dregs of society – a police station [with] petty sessions is just outside … checking the lawless inhabitants'.[70] Some commons were stated to have been assembly points for rebels in 1798 – Fossy, Co. Offaly, and Forth Hill, Wexford.[71] Where else would rebels have assembled – on the front lawn of the local landlord's residence? Having completely ignored the welfare of those families who had been forced off the land by enclosure or otherwise, and were thereby left homeless, landless and crowded onto marginal property bereft of the normal social constraints of managed estates, it is not surprising that the legislators viewed them negatively. Yet the consequences of turning people onto the roadside in great numbers had also been brought to the notice of legislators.[72] In the midst of their appalling living conditions, there were many positive signs of the ditch-dwellers and cabin-dwellers rising above adversity. Countering the bad name given to squatters at Forth mountain, a Wexford official stated that far from harbouring outlaws and fugitives the priorities for the 'quiet and peaceable' squatters was to get a school-house for their children. In another context it was asserted that the children of squatters, 'idle fellows', had become industrious.[73] The evidence received by the royal commission on the poorer classes in Ireland from north Co. Dublin in the mid-1830s summed the situation up concisely:

> On the common of Balscaddan and the bog of the Ring … the march of improvement … is to be seen … from the sod hut of the new squatter, trembling for ejection, to the neat whitewashed and well-plastered cottage of the old settler who now enjoying the full security of his tenure thinks only of improving his property.[74]

Following the Reform act of 1832,[75] many squatters sought registration as parliamentary electors as a gateway to respectability and an access to political power. Such registration was often opposed by officialdom. At Forth mountain many of the hundred squatters registered.[76] At Navan, attempts by encroachers to register were successfully resisted by the portreeve. A higher profile case was that of James Doyle, a squatter of Ballymore Eustace, who appealed the rejection of his application and won his appeal.[77]

During the period of active enclosure, the overall effect of legislation was to assist property owners to enclose commons while protecting them from the conflicting interests of landless peasants. In some English enclosure acts provision was made for allotments for the poor – those without rights of common or those without proof of rights, but there is no evidence of this having happened here.[78] It is arguable that the social distress caused by enclosure stemmed not from the specific fact of enclosing the ground, but rather from the prevailing philosophy as regards who should take profit from land. This was reflected in the balance which was maintained between property rights and social need, between legality and equity.

COUNTY DUBLIN

As elsewhere, in medieval times every manor in Co. Dublin had its commons. There are 27 townlands in Co. Dublin whose names contain the word 'commons',[79] yet only a small percentage of common lands are perpetuated in modern townland names. For example in Kill parish, Co. Dublin, alone, six commons have been documented: Dromin, Drinamore, Monolough and Tipperstown, all in the Brennanstown-Leopardstown area, at Roches Hill commons (a name still remembered) near Killiney, and, a commons for sourcing pottery clay, at Polloughs (*pollach*, a place full of holes) near Kill-of-the Grange village. Yet none of these six toponyms preserved 'commons' as a townland name.[80] Furthermore, almost certainly further commons existed which were never documented. F.H.A. Aallen states that the rural environs of Dublin were probably enclosed well before 1700. Yet much enclosure of commons also occurred in the 18th and 19th centuries.[81]

The largest landowners of Co. Dublin were institutional: the archbishop of Dublin, the cathedral of Christ Church and the crown. From the time of the reformation, *c.*1540 to the 19th century, there was relatively little change geographically in the lands in Co. Dublin of the archbishop of Dublin. Much of his control had been lost however through short-term management practices such as customary tenures, and long or reversionary leases.[82] A combination of widely scattered estates under an absentee landlord, of lost control, of little or no income being derived from the lands and in later times, a statutory prohibition on long leases of ecclesiastical lands, may explain why successive archbishops took no steps to enclose the common

land, thus allowing many of them to survive into a period where impoverished squatters were more likely to occupy them than were adjoining
tenants deadlocked by conflicting interests. The three areas around Dublin
where encroachment by squatters was most concentrated, Ballymore Eustace
(then in Co. Dublin), Swords, and Dalkey, as well as other areas of lesser
encroachment, were on the archbishop's estates. No doubt some of his major
tenants also utilized the management vacuum to encroach, though this would
not leave the same tell-tale clues on the landscape as would the jumble of
squatters' holdings.

Few records of commonage remain in relation to Christ Church
cathedral lands, but 16th- and 17th-century references to making ditches,
planting of trees on ditches, existence of 'parks' and covenanted improvements all point towards the replacement without apparent controversy, of
the old manorial farming by the new managed estates.[83]

There were four royal manors, the larger two at Newcastle Lyons and
Saggart, the smaller at Crumlin and at Esker near Lucan. They exceeded
12,000 acres in extent,[84] and it was not until the early 17th century that the
crown sought to replace with leases the copyhold tenure of the manorial
system. Newcastle Lyons had 80 acres of common until around 1829, with a
further 200 acres in the adjoining townland of Hazlehatch, Co. Kildare. It
retained, into the 18th century, the open field system of individually
cultivated strip holdings and shared pasturage at places like Shiskeen (marshy)
Common, for the villagers' livestock contained in a single herd.[85]

A surviving record of the community-based manor courts of Crumlin
for the period 1592–1600 gives us a few vignettes of the administration of
common land. In 1593, a new ordinance was passed rationing the available
grazing on the commons among the individual tenants and cottagers,
authorizing the seizing of excess cattle pending receipt of undertakings
from their owners and the levying of fines. The manor's animals were kept
as a single herd, shepherded by a single herdsman supported by commoners
in proportion to their stock numbers.[86] A number of commoners were
subsequently fined for over-grazing, for not co-operating with the herd, or
for not supplying him with food and drink as required. John and Patrick
Hoyle were charged with abusing their right of turbary by cutting for
commercial sale as fuel on the Dublin market, the furze bushes grown on
the commons for community use. John Hoyle was a misfit and a maverick:
he was also caught grazing animals illicitly on the commons; he allowed his
pigs to destroy the surface of the common by nuzzling the turf with unringed
snouts; he failed to reinstate the surface by harrowing and smoothing when
ordered and he was fined for assault and bloodshed on Robert Gosson. His
wife, Alison White, apparently a kindred character, made affray, assault and
bloodshed on Margaret Beagan.[87] Despite his shortcomings, John was elected
a constable in 1596, while both Patrick and John Hoyle later participated as

jurors. It appears that the network of responsibilities and rights of the inhabitants of Crumlin manor still operated according to ancient 'custom and practice' around the year 1600. Later, Crumlin Common was additionally used for sports, notably hurling and horse racing.[88] This commons had originally consisted of 150 acres.[89] In 1735 and 1751, bills for its enclosure were considered but rejected by the Irish house of commons; its enclosing act was not passed until after the act of Union, in 1818.[90] Contemporary surviving court records for Esker make scant reference to the day-today administration of their commons, though their descriptions of property 'also of all curtillages, gardens, orchards, free warrens, commons, pastures, and all other profits, commodities and easements', indicate the continuation of manor tenures around 1600.[91] In contrast to Crumlin, powerful land-holders rather than the community controlled affairs.[92]

Urban Dublin, like other large towns, maintained a number of commons for the benefit of its citizens. Such commons included Hoggen (much later College) Green, a pleasure ground and grazing area, the Steine (at the top of Pearse Street) a pasture and marsh, St Stephen's Green, a common pasture, Little Green (at Green Street), another common pasture, Oxmantown Green, a large grazing area, and St Kevin's Common at Camden Row (already broken up for tillage in 1223). The city's assembly in 1577 reserved the grazing at Hoggen Green, St Stephen's Green and Oxmantown Green for the livestock of free citizens only, and as late as 1635 they passed a law prohibiting the leasing of any part of them, so as to preserve them wholly for the use of the citizens and others 'to walke and take the open aire'.[93] Nevertheless some 17 acres of what remained of St Stephen's Green were sold off in 1664 as 86 building lots (19 of them drawn by members of the allocating committees). This left the green at its present size.[94] Hoggen Green was enclosed for institutional buildings, Trinity College, Cary's Hospital (later Chichester House and now the Bank of Ireland) and a Bridewell.[95] Oxmantown Green became the home of the Blue–Coat school, the Royal (Collins) Barracks and the Smithfield markets, while the city sold off 99 building lots there in 1665.

Unusually for Ireland, Finglas had a village green. In the year 1702 the parish vestry agreed to the levelling and tree planting of the village pound to provide a recreation green, following the removal of the pound to a 'big green' near Cardiff's Bridge. The proposal was subject to a guarantee by its initiator Philip Prosser, that the recreation ground would always be open to the public and would never be enclosed. This implies that the villagers saw enclosure as a potential threat to what appears to have been a newly-created common. A May pole was located on the green until the 1840s when the Finglas May Fair was discontinued through the efforts of an enthusiastic cleric, Fr Henry Young.[96] Across the city, the site of Donnybrook Fair, situated between the village and the river Dodder, was most likely a commonage at an early date. It was located on manor lands, it was on the flood-plain of a river, and it was either 'waste land' or rough pasture, being used for a fair ground during the crop-growing season. Dublin also had many other suburban commons which cannot be dealt with here.[97]

The Dublin Society's statistical survey at the start of the 19th century listed some 25 areas containing 2,560 acres which remained as common lands. This report advocated their enclosure, arguing that their utility could be thereby enhanced tenfold. Lieutenant Archer, its author, pointed out as a model for repeating, the recent successful enclosure, draining and planting of 500 acres of mountain above Rathfarnham. However, he anticipated vandalism and stealing of crops by locals because of 'poverty and idleness', but expressed confidence that enclosure would eventually lead to a more prudent demeanour in the lower classes and hoped that they would see their folly when provisions would become cheaper.[98]

Over the next 20 years or so, statutory powers to enclose various commons within Co. Dublin were sought by their neighbouring proprietors. In 1803 Garristown commons was enclosed.[99] In 1804 enclosure of Donabate and Portrane commons was approved.[100] More noticeably, in 1816, a group of Co. Dublin landowners announced plans to enclose commons at Kilmainham, Clondalkin, Fox and Geese, Crumlin, Bray, Newcastle, Hazelhatch, Shiskeen, Ballinascorney, Tallaght, Swords and Rathcoole, but no plans emerged.[101] However, landowners at Saggart, at Tallaght, Kilsallaghan and Lusk, and at Kilmainham, St James, Clondalkin, Crumlin, and Rathcoole proceeded on their own.[102] Meanwhile, 120 acres of Swords Commons were being settled on by strangers, while squatters in some numbers had colonized commons areas around Lusk, Balscaddan, Loughlinstown, Dalkey, Rathcoole and Newcastle as well as at Ballymore-Eustace.[103]

The year 1824 was eventful for commonage in the county. A local man, building a house on the Ballinascorney commons, complained to the assizes that 11 men known to him from childhood had arrived at night with 20 or 30 other men who were armed, and that they levelled the house. The defendants produced very good referees as to character, unlike the plaintiff who was shifty in his evidence, and the alleged attackers were discharged. But the case illustrates the emotion attached to encroachment, even where a well known local person of the same social class as the alleged objectors was concerned.[104] Furthermore, in April of that year, police had tried unsuccessfully to dislodge the commoners of Fox and Geese who then appealed to the lord lieutenant to prohibit a rumoured further raid by army or police to stop them grazing their cattle on the commons.[105]

2. Dalkey: squatters sell on to speculators

The lands of Dalkey were owned by the archbishop of Dublin, as lord of the manor of Shankill; the commons of Dalkey were specifically mentioned in an inquisition as early as 1611.[1] Thomas Reading's map of Dalkey, dated 1765, indicates the survival of the long narrow strip field pattern of an out-dated farming system.[2] Under this system, a burgage invariably included a house, garden, strips of arable land and grazing on the commons.[3] Reading's map also shows the commons, 123 acres Irish Plantation Measure (196 statute acres) in extent, lying to the south and east of the town.[4] It was known as Dalkey Stone Common because of an ancient dolmen and stone circle subsequently removed for building materials. A local ballad, 'The Kilruddery Hunt', used this description: 'At Dalkey stone common we had him in view … '[5] Peter Wilson, writing in 1768, says of the commons that it afforded 'most excellent pasture for sheep' and that it was also used by the poor to graze cattle. Fishing was an important local industry and crabs and lobsters were found on the rocky coast-line.[6]

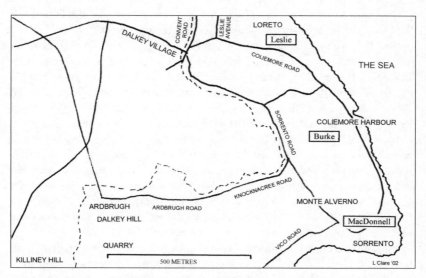

1 Location map – Dalkey Commons. The commons is to the right of the dotted line. The various sections of the commons are shown, together with the areas of interest of the three major speculators, Leslie, Burke and MacDonnell.

Mining for lead commenced on the commons at Sorrento around 1752, when smelting houses, a store yard and workmen's cabins were erected. The mines were never very successful and ceased production in 1793. The erection of buildings however, represented a breach of the inviolability of the commons.[7] When the miners moved out, the fishermen moved in and they and their descendents enclosed plots with rough stone walls, within which they planted potatoes.[8] Nevertheless, the squatters' cabins on the commons were few and far between. A writer in 1840 described the scene as it had been before the mass enclosure of plots. 'A few cottages stretching from the village along its southern boundary, and a solitary cabin originally built by miners and which still remains, were the only habitations to be seen'. Nostalgically, he added:

> the country along the southern shore of our beautiful bay, from Dun
> Leary to the lands-end at Dalkey common, presented a nearly
> uniform character of wildness and solitude – healthy grounds, broken
> only by masses of granite rocks, and tufts of blossomy furze, without
> culture, and except in the little walled villages of Bullock and Dalkey,
> almost uninhabited.[9]

The commons had other uses besides agriculture, fishing and mining. According to the 19th-century local author James Gaskin, Dublin city inhabitants had fled to Dalkey during a plague in 1575, and erected camps on the commons.[10] On a happier note, another writer described the numerous picnic parties of the middle classes enjoying the singing, the fiddle and the flute, and the happy dancers footing the Irish jig and country dance. He was personally invited to attend one of the rural fetes held by the higher ranks who arrived in open carriages, followed by innumerable parties of inferior ranks as onlookers. They assembled in a beautiful and extensive green amphitheatre and had the use of two marquees, one for the accommodation of the ladies and one for the dinner party. Two pleasure yachts of those who arrived by sea were moored nearby. Quadrille dancers moved to the music of a military band until the party broke up after sunset. There was not a single instance of rudeness or indecorum on the part of the uninvited spectators who remained at a distance.[11] More formally, but jocosely, an annual festival was held several times towards the end of the 18th century for the crowning of a king of Dalkey Island in a burlesque which attracted thousands of Dubliners to the commons and to Dalkey island. Due to the pre-revolutionary atmosphere of the time, however, the festival was abandoned in 1798.[12]

Although there were already a few houses occupied by fishermen, small farmers and labourers on the commons early in the 19th century, a dynamic was created around 1814 which would forever change the physical features of Dalkey hill, and lead to the almost total colonisation of the commons. In that year, Richard Toutcher the promoter of the concept of an asylum harbour at Dun Leary, was utterly frustrated by his failure to get permission

2 Dalkey village and commons, early 19th century – engraving.

from land owners to quarry rock free of charge for the project, a failure which could potentially kill off the scheme. But learning that lease-holders in Dalkey automatically secured as commoners, rights including quarrying rights, he personally leased 10 acres, paying over the odds to secure his foothold on the commons. He next persuaded his fellow commoner, Lord Carysfort, to join him in agreeing to the free use of the quarry for the project which, he argued would not only provide a safe haven for mariners but would also enhance the value of the Lord's local estate. Having secured Lord Carysfort's agreement, he used the lord's example to procure similar commitments from other commoners to permit, at no cost, the quarrying of stone for the harbour at Dun Leary from the Dalkey commons.[13]

Work on the harbour commenced in 1817 and travelling labour was attracted to the work available at the quarry and on the piers. Many settled in temporary dwellings at the edges of the commons, and in 1823 no less than 1,000 workers were stated to be living there without sanitary facilities or running water.[14] In April 1824, during the same month that the commoners of Fox and Geese commons, Clondalkin, were under threat, a petition was submitted to the lord lieutenant, on behalf of some 800 squatters, declaring 'the said commons are about, it seems, to be taken in, and [the] petitioners' little cabins are to be thrown down, by which means [the] petitioners and their unhappy and helpless families will be left quite destitute of shelter, in number about 800 people.' They begged to be left on the commons only as long as the quarrying work was continuing.[15]

Apparently successful proceedings were taken in 1824 to remove 46 squatters from the commons, but when the writs were lodged with Sir Henry Ribton, the county sheriff, for execution, he was unwilling to rely on the civil power for enforcement and he called for the military to come to its aid. When this situation came to the notice of General Sir George Cockburn of Shanganagh, he addressed a memorial to the lord lieutenant on behalf of the squatters, and the aid of the military was refused. The result was that the writs for eviction were never executed. Sir George's intervention can be considered to be the key turning point with regard to the enclosure of Dalkey commons, although in the light of the military's refusal to intervene at Ballymore Eustace in 1820 and 1821, he may have been pushing an open door. When it gradually dawned on the population that the writs would not be executed, additional cabins were thrown up and the parts of the commons not yet appropriated became occupied.[16]

The squatters were not a homogeneous group; the quarrymen generally located on the edges of the commons and were poorer than the owners of the potato plots. In one group of 29 holdings at the quarry, the largest hereditament was of only £5 valuation, and 22 cottages had no ground attached. Those squatters who can be identified as being either farmers or fishermen typically held a garden plot or plots totalling an acre or more in the heart of the commons near Coliemore or Sorrento. Some of these most likely predated the appearance of the quarrymen around 1817.[17] One interesting squatter was a Franciscan priest, Fr Francis Smyth, who in 1820 built a small oratory and a charitable school for upwards of a hundred of the quarrymen's children at Monte Alverno, a rocky hilltop site said to have been bequeathed to him. But who on the commons had a proprietary interest to bequeath in 1820? The schools and oratory appear to have closed between 1837 and 1848, and private residences were built on the land. The 'chapel house' became 'Kinross'.[18]

There was a wide range of people seeking wealth: the poor squatter seizing and holding his cabin plot, the squatter who sublet a portion of his acquired plot, the indigenous squatter who came into possession of a few plots, the outsider who secured a plot or two by squatting or buying in, the investor in a couple of squatted-on properties like the purchaser of two large houses at Sorrento Terrace, the larger speculator who bought out a number of small plots, the bigger investor who specialized in larger properties, the adjoining landlord who moved into the commons, the 'big three' speculators, Charles Leslie, Martin Burke and Richard MacDonnell and even the state through the Board of Ordnance.[19]

And who were the speculators and investors? The 'big three' are dealt with below, as is the adjoining landlord, Robert Warren of Killiney Hill. There were also substantial city lawyers, doctors and businessmen, like attorney-at-law Michael Carey, surgeon Richard Parkinson and George Foster cabinet-maker, all men of substantial wealth and some of whom became resident in the Dalkey area.[20] There was an indigenous publican, Pat Byrne, who was also described as a dairyman and a farmer, and there was a speculator, Gerald Tyrrell, a bookseller, who bought sites for development and sale or leasing.[21] And was the Francis Maguire, contractor and farmer, the same Francis Maguire who signed the squatters' petition against the throwing down of his little cabin over the heads of his helpless and unhappy family?[22]

The 1837 ordnance map indicates a linear development hugging the edge of the former commons, a pattern characteristic of a squatter settlement. Significantly Convent Road, part of Sorrento Road, Knocknacree Road and Ardbrugh Road together form a peripheral road which lies a few feet inside, and shadows the meandering boundary of the commons. This indicates that their origin was as a track serving the encroachers' plots strung along the peri-meter. And on the western side of Ardbrugh Road, at Dalkey Hill, a group of houses, separated by narrow footpaths and alleyways rather than by roadways, testifies that they occupy the sites of former unplanned squatters' plots.[23]

Leslie Avenue also shows signs of original unplanned development, but does not fit the pattern of a peripheral road. Convent Road and Leslie Avenue, both extremely narrow thoroughfares, may represent ancient track-ways between Dalkey town, Bulloch and Coliemore, which formed a wedge detached from the rest of the commons yet suitable for squatting on. However, Leslie built most of the small houses fronting Leslie Avenue, described by one account as gifts for employees and others, but possibly built to resettle squatters whom he had displaced.[24]

Following the collapse of efforts to remove the squatters in 1824, land speculators moved in to buy up the plots where squatters' rights had been secured after 20 years of unchallenged occupation. There were three main purchasers of these holdings. The earliest speculator into the field was Charles Leslie, a wholesale chemist of Bride Street, Dublin. From about 1828, he occupied land on the commons at Carrick-na-Greinne, subsequently part of Loreto Abbey. He consolidated his property by buying out neigh-bouring squatters' cabins. In 1842 he sold the site of Loreto Abbey to the sisters for £1,500.[25] It was later alleged that he paid only £18 for land which became worth many thousands of pounds.[26] The Revd Richard MacDonnell, provost of Trinity College, soon followed Leslie. He was buying up garden plots and the cliffs in the Sorrento area at knockdown prices in 1829. Three properties, which he bought from a mariner, a farmer and a spinster, cost £6, £6 10s. and £13 respectively.[27] MacDonnell's son, Hercules, later claimed that with the reduction in work available at the quarry as the harbour neared completion, many squatters were glad to take a payment and to move off. Hercules also claimed that there was astonish-ment and ridicule at a Fellow of Trinity College being so foolish as to build even a small summer cottage on 'so worthless a site'.[28] Richard subsequently lived in Sorrento House at the seaward end of Sorrento Terrace, while Hercules, a barrister, who developed Sorrento Terrace in 1845, lived at Sorrento Cottage.[29] A local man, Joseph Hempenstall, had written to the lord lieutenant in 1833, complaining that MacDonnell had bought 25 acres from an emigrating labourer, and had cut off public access to the sea.[30]

The third large speculator was Martin Burke, an entrepreneur, who successfully founded the Shelbourne Hotel. He had an address at Seapoint House, Monkstown. He entered the market in 1836, when he and his barrister son, James Milo Burke, paid much larger sums, but still objectively small amounts, £150, £317, £625, £215, £190, for larger plots in the Coliemore area, between Leslie's and MacDonnell's properties. On these lands Milo built large residences like Khyber Pass, Victoria House, Springfield, and Queenstown Castle.[31] Other land speculators acquired property in the potentially fashionable area around this time, including the Warren family who already owned the adjoining Killiney estate and who bought up the higher lands above the quarry, around the telegraph tower. A large fashionable new 'Town of Queenstown' to cover the entire Killiney and Dalkey Hill area was proposed in 1840, but never came to fruition.[32]

During the 1830s, the land speculation most likely thrived on the feelings of a coming property boom implied by the sight of the construction of the new Sorrento Terrace, the rumours of the proposed new town of Queenstown, and talk of the extension of the Dublin to Kingstown railway as far as Dalkey.[33] By the 1850s, following the opening of this railway link to the city, the commons area was becoming the home of businessmen, legal, academic and other professionals, living on individual sites bought directly from squatters or on subdivisions of land bought by speculators. Some residences were being let out for the summer season.[34] However, many squatters' plots were not purchased for high-class redevelopment, as evidenced by the large number of individual houses on small garden plots which can still be seen on the former commons.

In its original condition, the open commons provided a network of mountain tracks for getting from place to place. While its enclosure produced a peripheral route along the line of the Ardbrugh, Knocknashee and part of Sorrento roads, the claiming of private ownership tended to close off the old throughways. The main elements of the framework of tracks were along the lines of the present Sorrento Road, Coliemore Road and Vico Road. Sorrento Road is shown on pre-enclosure maps as a track leading to the mines. According to Hercules MacDonnell, the owner of the Sorrento area, there had at first been only a rugged trackway for a short distance beyond Dalkey village leading towards Sorrento, and to reach his father's place it was necessary to walk over rough stones and rocks and through mud and furze. MacDonnell at his own expense had widened the whole Sorrento Road from Dalkey Main Street and had laid the granite kerbing.[35] He also asserted that he had widened the narrow path on the line of the Vico Road as far as the end of his property. Warren, the owner of Killiney, had erected a boundary wall across the path of the Vico Road, which James Gaskin in 1869 described as 'the invidious wall at the end of the road [which] bars the progress of the lovers of nature's charms, along the curving shore of Killiney'. During a period of controversy in 1885, the Dalkey town commissioners were told that three of the four landowners whose permission was needed to build the Vico Road to Killiney had agreed to the scheme, namely Warren, Higgins and MacDonnell, while Lloyd of Victoria Lodge had still to give his consent. The Vico Road, with its connections to Killiney railway station and Killiney village, was eventually opened to the public by the lord lieutenant on 3 June 1889, following a procession of coaches carrying the celebrities of Dublin and district. This cavalcade was specially organized and decorated for the occasion by William James Talbot Power. It was described as the prettiest spectacle ever witnessed by lovers of horseflesh. The celebrations were marred however by most disagreeable weather.[36]

The early maps show no track running directly from the town of Dalkey along the coast to Coliemore, though Wilson's account of 1768 mentions the 'remains of a very strong causeway that runs across part of the commons and was evidently calculated to facilitate the carriage of goods between the coast and the town'. These remains would have dated from the time when Dalkey sound had been not only the port of Dalkey, but a port for Dublin.[37] Today's small Coliemore harbour is modern, having been commenced in 1847 by Burke and MacDonnell and completed in 1868.[38] The encroachments on the commons did not close off the access to Coliemore, but the roadway beyond the harbour towards Sorrento Terrace, despite the development of the area, remained as a rough passage through the middle decades of the 1800s and only became a public road around 1886.[39]

The controversy over the opening up of the area with public roads was mild compared with the tension engendered by the closing off of old trackways, particularly to the shore and to bathing places, and by the cutting off, by high boundary walls, of the views over the bay. One of the earliest causes of dissent related to the spring or well on Charles Leslie's land. Leslie had closed off the former rights-of-way to the shore and to the well. A woman named Cullen, a returned emigrant, is said to have asserted her rights to use the well and Leslie settled her claim by providing her with a house on Leslie Avenue, and by building a subterranean passage under his grounds, both to the well and to the shore. The well became known as Lady Cullen's well, and later Lady well and Our Lady's well, although it had no traditional religious significance.[40]

The questions of enclosure, blocking of rights-of-way and ending of public recreation on the commons, became a political issue in the local elections of 1885. The *Freeman's Journal* slated the 'rapacious men' who built the finest mansions with private tennis courts, hidden by high granite walls. It spoke of 'public plunder' and 'land grabbing' with 'conscience money' paid for ground obtained. It abhorred the 'wall extensions and fancy gates' blocking off passageways. It decried the loss of a potential magnificent esplanade from Loreto Convent to Sorrento Cape and alleged that one sea-shore mansion stood on ground bought for a gallon of whiskey from a 'vender' whose descendents still lived nearby, while another site cost two gallons of porter plus 4s. 6d.[41]

Specific locations of blocked-off pathways were given, mostly to the sea-shore but also to the Lady well. Encroachments on Torca Road were also condemned. Public access to bathing places had been stopped, and private piers had been built on the public shore. Finally the paper strongly criti-cized the Dalkey town commissioners, some of them land speculators, for not resisting laneway closures.[42]

The only 'guilty' land-owner who comprehensively responded was Hercules MacDonnell of Sorrento. He pointed out that his father had originally come to a derelict, unfashionable area, that he had done nothing illegal, that there were no rights-of-way within his area and that he had done the public a service by investing in roads in the area. The other named residents generally challenged the existence of rights-of-way, and claimed that vandalism, dumping and other nuisances made the fencing off of laneways necessary.[43]

A public meeting was called 'to consider the best means to recover the rights of the people to the foreshore of Dalkey'. The police were on the alert, but the rally, chaired by Edward Field TC and attended by 300 people, passed off peacefully. There was much rhetoric and nostalgia about previous freedom to roam the commons. However, little progress was made, apart from an offer from Milo Burke to re-open a blocked-off laneway, and news of a possible opening up of Vico Road. A motion was passed calling for renewed access to the shore and the public wells.[44] The police had a constable on duty on the commons to stop direct action but none was taken.[45] The town commissioners, goaded into action, devoted much time to the issue of access but they had little power to act. They wrote to the landowners involved, with little success. The only practical result was a decision to purchase the land for the small public park between Coliemore Road and the sea. Sorrento Park nearby, was donated permanently to public use by Lady MacDonnell in 1894.[46]

We see therefore that in Dalkey, the commons was lost to public use through a series of events starting with the decision to build Dun Leary harbour, followed in succession by the securing by sleight of hand of the quarrying rights at Dalkey, the settlement of quarrymen in large numbers along the boundaries of the commons, the abortive attempt to evict them before they would secure squatters rights, the wholesale squatting which followed the realization that the existing squatters were being allowed to stay put, the moving-in of land speculators large and small, and the eventual consolidation of the recently-privatized properties. Yet the partitioning of the commons took place peacefully, though lubricated by money changing hands. Not all attempts to enclose the commons were so peaceful, as will soon become apparent.

3. The Sugar Loaves: seizures by squires spark off sedition

While the complete enclosure of both Dalkey and Bray commons was accomplished within clearly defined and limited periods, the process has been in progress around Kilmacanogue over centuries and was alleged to be still going on in recent times.[1] Consequently the study of the commonage around the Co. Wicklow village, restricts its focus to specific events within a limited period, while aiming to illustrate different approaches to enclosure. The parish of Kilmacanogue falls geographically into three distinct sections: the demesne land to the north including the townlands of Wingfield, Hollybrook, Charleville, Tinnehinch, Ballyorney, Stylebawn and Fasseroe; the fertile valley of Glencormick, Kilmacanogue and Kilmurray straddling the N11 between the two Sugar Loaves, and the upland area rising from Kilmacanogue village, through the Rocky Valley, to the plateau of Calary and the summit of the Big Sugar Loaf. The Little Sugar Loaf, though separated by a valley, belongs to the upland area. This upland section geographically incorporates a few adjoining townlands from Calary and

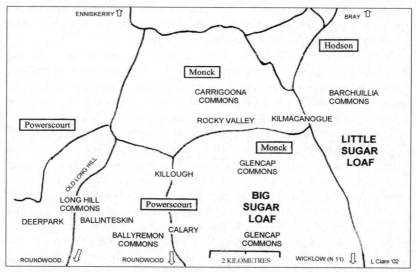

3 Location map – The commons around Kilmacanogue. The spheres of interest of the three major landlords, Powerscourt, Monck and Hodson are indicated.

Powerscourt parishes. Though grants of land were recorded in the area during the reign of Charles I, the ownership of the entire area was not clearly defined and by the 1830s, the local landlords, successors in title to recipients of land grants from the king, were doubtful as to their exact rights. Consequently, the earl of Rathdowne (Viscount Monck) of Charleville, Viscount Powerscourt of Powerscourt Demesne and Sir George Hodson of Hollybrook, Bray, signed a deed of partition on 3 December 1839, dividing between them, certain areas of upland commonage, mainly in Kilmacanogue parish.[2] This deed is dealt with below. There are nine hilly townlands incorporating the name 'commons' and there is evidence that there were other commons in the district outside these nine townlands.[3]

The process of investing to improve the productivity of the mountainous heath and bogland by enclosing, clearing rocks and stones, draining, fencing, planting and erecting buildings has been continuing in the area over an extended period. Arthur Young who stayed at Newtownmountkennedy and Tinnehinch in 1776, and who passed along the Glen of the Downs, noted that considerable tracts of mountain had already been improved.[4] The Dublin Society's statistical survey of 1801 praised Lord Powerscourt for converting some of his upper lands 'from being covered with heath and boulders of granite … into one of the finest sheep walks … anywhere observed', but noted the vast tracts of still unimproved land in the neighbourhood. This perhaps reflects the description in 1788 of the 64 square-mile 'completely uninhabited' plateau between Calary and Glendalough, 13 miles from the city, with '400 acres let here at a guinea annually'.[5] It appears reasonable to apply the Dublin Society's comments regarding conditions in Powerscourt parish to neighbouring Kilmacanogue and Calary.[6]

There was considerable poverty in the district. The main landlords typically leased to large tenants, who in turn sub-leased to labourers or small holders. Sub-tenants of large farmers paid a fair rent, but those who rented from petty farmers paid up to three times the real value.[7] In 1796, the Revd M. Sandys of Powerscourt wrote to Henry Grattan pointing out what he knew already, that even in most favourable circumstances of health, weather and availability of constant employment, a labourer was uncertain of his ability to support his family. A generation later the land-owners of Delgany objected to rating arrangements for the new Rathdown poor law union, because they were already 'carrying the burden of the very poor parish of Kilmacanogue'.[8]

The quality of housing reflected the general poverty of the area. Young held that some of the cabins in Wicklow were worse than any in Connacht, and he had described cottiers generally as living in miserable looking hovels … one room only … mud and straw walls … one door, no window or chimney … thatched with straw, potato stalks or heath …[9] The statistical survey costed 'the mud or sods formed to prop up a roof of miserable thatch that hardly defends them from the falling rain and often permeable in every breeze' as between £1 10s. and £2.[10]

4 Old Long Hill/Ballinteskin ridge in middle distance, with Killough and Glencap Commons in foreground.

Encroaching by poor people on the commons was endemic. Kilmacanogue was one of the a number of areas of east Leinster where unenclosed inferior country became populated by landless cottiers and labourers getting seasonal employment and growing a few potatoes.[11] In 1841, 40 per cent of Kilmacanogue parish's entire stock of houses were still one-roomed mud cabins.[12] It is clear that living space was at a premium, which explains the gradual colonisation of the commons by the homeless. An analysis of *Griffith's Valuation*, published ten years later, for Kilmacanogue parish and for five adjoining townlands of Calary parish, shows that 135 occupiers, 95 per cent of all the local suspected squatters, (those with small holdings claiming freehold ownership), lived in townlands whose names contained the word 'commons'. Of these occupiers, 26 had no land at all, 71 held less than an acre, 21 held between one and two acres and 17 possessed over two acres. A few occupants held more than one plot. Furthermore, of these 135 'squatters', 99 had houses on their plots, 85 per cent of which were valued at less than £1 per annum. In Longhill Commons, the average valuation of houses was 7s. 2d.; the highest valuation was 8s. 0d. This gives a measure of the poor quality of the housing erected on the commons.

THE BIG SUGAR LOAF, BALLINTESKIN

Virtually all the opposition to enclosing the local commons was directed at Lord Powerscourt. It centred on the four adjoining townlands of Ballinteskin, Long Hill Commons, Killough and Ballyremon Commons which lie to the west of the Big Sugar Loaf. The [Old] Long Hill, had been described by a traveller from Enniskerry to Roundwood in 1834 as 'wild and uninteresting country but obviously under improvement [with] more than one substantial farmhouse newly built, or in course of building'.[13] Yet in 1840, other travellers described the road as

> A dreary and uninteresting road running nearly all the way through an arid and unproductive common. There are a few miserable hovels now and then skirting the wayside with wretched patches of shrivelled potatoes planted in bits of land, the forcing of which into comparative cultivation can scarcely recompense the very extreme poverty.[14]

By 1842, the large Ballyremon commons already had much arable land. Some improvements were then going on; other improvements had been carried out in the past. Significantly a large proportion of the 'moorey green pasture [was] much injured by soil being carried off [as turf or peat]'.[15] The previous availability of such a source of free fuel, as well as land for free grazing, may supply reasons why the local populace generally, as well as the people squatting there, would be so protective of the commons if large-scale enclosure appeared imminent. The fear may have been increased with the opening up of the area to 'improvement' by the construction in the 1830s of the new road from Kilmananogue through the Rocky Valley and Calary to the village of Roundwood. A Church of Ireland parish with a new church and parish school had also been established in that decade, indicating the expansion of development in the area.[16]

Community relations were already on edge; the location of Kilmacanogue chapel, on a marginal site within the commons, was itself symbolic of religious tensions.[17] The 1798 rising, some 40 years before the attempted enclosure, was still within living memory. There had been 31 societies of the United Irishmen in the Powerscourt area, including one which appears to have been based at the Old Long Hill and which had among its members men of the same surnames as participants in the opposition to enclosure. Insurgent leader Joseph Holt had lived close by at Mullinaveigue. Peter Burke, schoolteacher of Long Hill commons, recruited actively for the United Irishmen in the Kilmacanogue area until he was captured and executed on the sea commons at Bray. Viscounts Monck and Powerscourt had organized the military response. Brother Luke Cullen recorded many atrocities of the yeomanry in the general area. The insurgents were badly mauled a few miles away at the battle of Newtownmountkennedy. Within the community there had been supporters of both sides.[18] On 8 July 1832, a reported 20,000 people had met on Glencap Commons overlooking Calary to hold an anti-tithe meeting, and although this was not simply a local event, the selected venue indicates a level of local political awareness.[19] More importantly, in the late 1830s there were a number of local incidents of intimidation and physical attack, mainly with regard to disputes over property. In Powerscourt parish, in 1838, seven cabins from which the occupants had been evicted were torched; another was pulled down; threatening letters, either unsigned or from 'Captain Rock', promised death to their recipients; one recipient fled to England and the house he had vacated was burnt down before the new tenant from Glencullen could take possession. On Long Hill Commons, publican Elijah Sutton's house was burnt down the night after he had been stopped from ploughing part of a commons opposite his door by a neighbour claiming an equal right to plough.[20]

Such was the context of tension and strife in which Powerscourt commenced a campaign to enclose the commons. Its course may well mirror similar efforts elsewhere. The Powerscourts had been gradually 'improving' their estate by taking in formerly unproductive land. The marginalized population were pushed away to the uplands, but as enclosure continued, the day came when their presence on even the most marginal lands obstructed the path of further progress. In 1831 while Richard, the sixth viscount, was still a minor, ejectment proceedings were first issued.[21] Similar proceedings followed in 1834 when it was considered necessary to call in a troop of dragoons to implement a sheriff's warrant putting Lord Powerscourt into possession. Although possession was given to Powerscourt on that day, the following day the people were back in their houses and they remained there.[22] A year after he came of age in 1836, Richard moved to enclose new parts of the commons and urged Sandys his agent to canvass the long term squatters to persuade them to take 'nominal leases of seven years in the three names'. He realized that he was moving into undefined territory, literally as well as metaphorically, and asked Sandys to seek prior agreement for further enclosures from Henry Monck, Lord Rathdowne, and Sir George Hodson, the other major landlords of the area. By the end of 1838, he anticipated having to buy off Rathdowne and eleven months later he directed that the land should be surveyed and a formal deed of partition drawn up.[23] This deed, dated 3 December 1839, divided up some 1370 Irish acres of common. Powerscourt got 618 acres, mainly on the upper northern slope of the Big Sugar Loaf, and in the Killough, Ballinteskin, Long Hill and Ballyremon Commons areas. Rathdowne secured 602 acres, at Carrigoona and the Rocky Valley and on the southern slope of the Big Sugar Loaf. Hodson received 149 acres at Bohilla commons on the Little Sugar Loaf.[24] Within three weeks Sandys had issued a circular to squatters signed 'your obedient servant' but notifying them of the partitioning and calling them in to the estate office to 'make arrangements ... which may be satisfactory to all parties'.[25] His rapid response was apparently not sufficiently speedy for Powerscourt, who urged him to set the commons 'soon' on the basis of a seven-year lease at 'half-a-crown an acre', the tenant to fence and keep under cultivation.[26]

Lord Powerscourt put aside certain lands to resettle some 'poor people' while he moved to clear a tract of commonage for other purposes. Marking out of Lord Powerscourt's new enclosure adjoining his deerpark at Ballinteskin (appropriately meaning 'the homestead of the waste ground') on the Old Long Hill started on Friday, 29 May 1840, and on the following Sunday evening his agent, Robert Sandys, stated that he (Sandys) had been visited by a Catholic workman who had told him that at the chapel that day, the priest had called on the congregation 'as men to prevent [the fencing] and to pull level all that was done'. Sandys was told that the priest was to hold a station at 12 o'clock on the next day 'for the purpose of having what was done [undone], and of course giving absolution and praise to those who played the most active part'. Sandys placed men on watch at the site in anticipation of the 'regular priest–ridden gang who must obey'.[27]

'High–noon' arrived on Monday 1 June 1840, and some 150 men arrived, armed with spades and shovels under the apparent leadership of one Garret Toole of Kilmacanogue. When he approached the new ditch, William Booth of the Deerpark, Lord Powerscourt's land bailiff, called on him in the name of Queen Victoria to desist, but within a few minutes, the fence or ditch was levelled and wilfully destroyed. No resistance was offered. A number of the trespassers were identified by Lord Powerscourt's men.[28] The word was out that a much bigger crowd would arrive the following Monday, and Sandys sought police protection against 'the great spirit of insubordination'. An assurance that 50 police would be brought together on the next Sunday evening was given but it was specifically stated – and repeated ad nauseam over the next weeks – that while the police would foil any breach of the peace they would not be used to prevent the levelling of the fences.[29]

On Monday evening 8 June, the resident magistrate, Sir William Lynar of Kingstown, reported to headquarters that at noon that day, some 300 to 400 men appeared, advancing from Kilmacanogue and its neighbourhood. They were accompanied by a number of women and children and were again led by Garret Toole. Powerscourt's labourers had been instructed to 'fold up the skirts from their coats' to distinguish them from the mob. The police lined the road and the fence. When Lynar and Sandys approached the mob and enquired what they wanted, Toole replied that he came in the name of the queen to take possession of his property, and demanded to know what had brought the police there. Garret indeed had a point: the O'Tooles had been in possession of the manor of Powerscourt until it was forfeited to the crown by another Garrett O'Toole in 1603 when the Wingfield (Powerscourt) family took possession. In addition, Dermot McEdmund O'Toole and Ferroll McTirleach O'Toole both of Kilmacanogue lost their lands at the same time.[30] On Garret Toole's instruction, the mob rushed the works. Sandys remonstrated with the menacing and riotous crowd. Thomas Kennedy of Kilmacanogue 'in a very insolent and threatening manner', demanded that Lord Powerscourt's title deeds be read out to the mob, to which Sandys responded, rather naïvely suggesting that if the crowd dispersed and appointed a suitable person to meet the viscount's solicitor, they would have full information, but the way they were acting was not the way to try their title. Sandys further counselled the mob that someone was advising them badly, to which Kennedy, replied with a certain clarity, 'Damn all informers'. The magistrate reported all this to Dublin Castle adding that Powerscourt's men appeared to be in league with the mob. They fell back when the mob started to demolish the ditch and refused to obey their orders, and some were seen shaking hands with the rioters. The mob used much insulting and abusive language, directing their greatest abuse against the landlords, and they dared the police to fire. They vowed to return as often as necessary to level the fence; they gave three cheers and marched off. Some 35 names were noted of men who could be identified. The police were then dispersed to their stations. Garret Toole was charged with assault before a full bench of magistrates. The proceedings involved the rights and wrongs of the enclosure, although these were irrelevant to the actual case. Eventually Toole was discharged.[31] Given the potential risks, it took considerable courage on the part of the leaders to stand up publicly against the enclosure, particularly those who lived not on the commons but as tenants of Powerscourt or his larger lessees. That they did so also indicates the strong feelings among the people of the area.

The action next moved a kilometre or two away, to the western slopes of the Big Sugar Loaf. Alice Keane, a widow, assisted by a group of men, had fenced in a plot on the commons at Killough (pronounced Kill-ogue locally) and erected a hut overnight, in the widespread but mistaken belief that if it was completed before morning, a right to remain would be created. Proceedings for ejectment were pursued jointly by Lord Rathdowne, Lord Powerscourt and Sir George Hudson, the three signatories of the deed of partition dividing up the commons. They were heard at Wicklow assizes before a grand jury. The prosecution urged the judge not to countenance the spirit of lawlessness which would acquire possession of land by brute force. The jury found against the defendants with sixpence costs. This was regarded as a test case by both landowners and people. It was stated later that the three landlords had paid a total of £640 to pursue this sample case; to counter this a collection to fund the defence in both the civil and the associated criminal case, was taken up in the local national school.[32]

Also at the assizes, nine local men, including Toole and Kavanagh, were charged with making an affray and riot and with levelling fences at Killough on the day after the melee at Ballinteskin. The defendants pleaded guilty, but one of them addressed the court stating that they had grazing rights on the commons and had the authority of a resident magistrate to keep the fences levelled. The presiding judge responded that no one could use great force or violence to protect any right, and emphasized that the decision made no comment on the rights or wrongs of the dispute over the commons. The defendants were fined only six pence but were bound to the peace for five years.[33]

Further levelling of the fences at Ballinteskin took place on the morning and on the evening of 25 July, when small groups of men led by Thomas Kavanagh and by Patrick Rossiter levelled the fences under construction with their bare hands. Sandys noted that some of the levellers had already been bound to the peace. Perhaps it was because of the judge's advice in the Killough case that 'no one in the land had a right to support with great force or violence any right whatsoever' that they came in small numbers and worked only with their bare hands. The Powerscourt workmen outnumbered the trespassers on these occasions but in accordance with instructions they offered no resistance.[34]

And there were signs of a widening interest in the events. Mr Henry Grattan, a local magistrate and son of the patriot and orator, had visited the site on 26 July and informed his Lordship's workmen that he habitually passed there for the last ten years with his wife, family and dogs and he claimed a right of way. And a week later an attorney named Gard or Garde arrived with Kavanagh and others and instructed them to level the ditch again.[35] More demolition of fences occurred on dates later in August.[36] Sandys was also escalating the issue. He secured a temporary police station to be located near the disputed fence; he took legal advice as to possible proceedings against the trespassers for breaching their undertakings to the assizes. However, he ignored the advice not to proceed. He was apprehensive that the full bench of magistrates would attend the case and divide on political lines. He therefore petitioned the lord lieutenant, to appoint a stipendiary or professional magistrate to take the case, but he refused.[37]

At Enniskerry petty sessions early in September, more than 70 persons were charged with riotous assembly and assaults at Ballinteskin, on various dates in August. Mr Gard was described as driving up on a jaunting car, and calling on the workmen to stop erecting the fences. He asked Thomas Kavanagh who accompanied him what was to be done and Kavanagh said 'it must come down' with which Gard agreed. Two hours later men came up and demolished the fence. Early on 10 August, Laurence Rossiter led six men in a further levelling, allegedly also assaulting Henry Bolton, one of Powerscourt's men. Rossiter was alleged to be paying the demolishers seven shillings per week, and Henry Grattan was also alleged to be paying men to demolish the fences at a rate of 1s. per week more that Powerscourt was paying for their erection. The bench was composed of 11 resident magistrates, the greatest number ever assembled in Wicklow; three landowners with interests in the commons also attended but took no part in the proceedings. After an adjournment, Christopher Fitzsimon the chairman (a son-in-law

of Daniel O'Connell) discharged the men, begged them to conduct themselves peacefully in future, and told them not to view the discharge as the
establishment of their right. Four of the 11 magistrates dissented. From the
list of magistrates and the voting pattern, it is clear that the magistrates
divided along political lines, as Sandys had feared.[38]

There were some political recriminations in the aftermath of the case. Four
magistrates, Fitzsimon, two Grattans and Richard Greydon, were alleged to
have attended Bray chapel when a collection for defraying the defence was
made, an allegation which the Grattans at least denied. Earlier, the conservative
Evening Packet had seen the event as the beginning of a guerrilla war in one of
the few parts of the country where the law was respected by the peasantry.
They were 'encouraged by the Romish priests and the prospects of a parliament in College Green, under the control of the dictator Daniel O'Connell'.
Across the political and religious divide, the *Freeman's Journal* wrote emotional
editorials, inter alia stating that if Powerscourt had got away with the enclosure, the chapel at Kilmacanogue could have been at threat as it was sited on
a commons. Moreover, Powerscourt had blocked a right-of-way, forcing
Catholics to make a detour of a mile to pray in the dirty thatched barn in
Enniskerry, having refused them a half-an-acre of land for a chapel.[39]

Lord Powerscourt spent much of his time abroad, but kept in close
contact by post. Immediately after the major confrontation of 8 June 1840,
Powerscourt had written from London urging Sandys to make one more
enclosure attempt. He should recruit all the farmers and their sons for
building the fence, privately promising each a rent reduction in return for
their support and telling them that as Protestants it was their battle as much
as his. He should, moreover, offer a few of the best labourers an extra £1 if
they stuck to their fencing work so as to let the others begin their assault,
but warning them that they would be turned out of their work if they
failed. Any tenants not on lease who opposed the work should be served
immediately with eviction notices. This planned further showdown appears
not to have taken place. Later in the same month he wrote, 'I hope you will
see that no precaution is omitted for ensuring the conviction of those
rascals'; in July, 'If we succeed at the trials, I would divide the commons in
three good farms of 80 acres each and divide the rest in small portions to
the occupiers'; in October, 'an action might lie against [the magistrates] for
not granting informations' (to allow cases to proceed). At the same time he
also wrote:

> With regard to the rest, if you proceed with the ejectments you must
> not let the men so ejected to stay on the land, and have their huts
> pulled down at once. If we succeed in enclosing, we will build good
> substantial houses for new and good men.[40]

On 31 March 1841, Lord Powerscourt wrote to squatters over his printed signature, addressing them as 'friends', expressing a sincere desire for their welfare, and ending with 'I am, your well-wisher'. In his circular he stressed his own rights, referring to their breaches of the peace and saying that he had originally intended to let them stay on the land with all the privileges of the oldest tenants. He sought a peaceful agreement, 'foreseeing the melancholy consequences to you all, should you be turned out of your houses as you are likely to be, and thrown helpless on the world'. He would make them comfortable in their homes at a purely nominal rent [thereby terminating their squatters' title]. Failing that, neither entreaties nor intimidation would avert the severest penalties of the law.[41] His policy was to initiate pilot proceedings against a few who would not agree to pay rent. He lost no time in bringing the first small group of cases for ejectment which it was stated could have affected nearly 2,000 people, presumably including knock-on effects,. Having being charged £79 legal expenses which they could not afford, the squatters reached a settlement with Lord Powerscourt. According to the partisan *Evening Packet* his heart melted when they sued for terms, he pardoned their transgressions instead of seeking eviction, and 'the poor deluded people are now showering down their prayers upon his noble house'.[42] This was no universal phenomenon, however, as further similar cases were soon to occur.

Richard, sixth Viscount Powerscourt, died aged 29 in August 1844, to be succeeded by his son, eight-year-old Mervyn. Within six months Sandys had been fired by his trustees. Between December 1845 and July 1846 there were at least three distinct instances of squatters being prosecuted for riot, assault and malicious trespass. The incidents were not on the same scale as the events of 1840, though a troop of dragoons had been brought in in January 1845 to enforce an eviction of squatters. The squatters claimed in their defence that they were merely protecting their own land and they objected to the use of the criminal law to try to establish a civil right. Though some jail sentences resulted, eventually the magistrates agreed that they had no jurisdiction to determine property rights.[43]

The squatters brought before the various Enniskerry petty sessions, found themselves in a very intimidating environment. The court was held in a gatelodge of Lord Powerscourt. Police armed with firelocks patrolled the area. On one occasion a sole magistrate arrived two hours late. On another, the defendants' solicitor, a reporter and the local priest, unlike the other 'gentlemen', were evicted by a policeman from the inner part of the court, an error which was later apologized for. The prosecution attorneys consulted the magistrates in chambers. Despite protests, one session was adjourned to a date when the defendants' counsel was scheduled to be away on circuit. Robert Sandys while sitting as a magistrate, was sworn and gave evidence, albeit on a non-controversial matter. Most of all, on one occasion, Captain Cranfield, Sandys' successor as Lord Powerscourt's agent, sat on the bench. Even when a professional magistrate presided, the non-professional, landowning magistrates participated in decisions by majority vote.[44]

It appears that Lord Powerscourt was the prime mover among the three parties to the partitioning of the commons. He made the running during the period prior to the signing of the deed of partition; he was the landlord who subsequently pressed ahead with enclosure; he took the legal actions; he ejected the tenants. Lord Rathdowne appears to have taken little initiative or action in this direction and much of his take is still a commons. Sir George Hodson occupied one parcel of 26 acres of Bohilla common without evidence of opposition, and left the rest in its original state. Despite the legal and economic pressures, at the end of the period studied, there were still numerous small plot-holders claiming freehold on the commons.[45] Further consolidation took place later, either through the efforts of Lord Powerscourt or the operations of the land commission.

THE LITTLE SUGAR LOAF, BOHILLA

Bohilla or Barchuillia ('top of the woods') Commons, lies mainly on the Kilmacanogue or western side of the Little Sugar Loaf. The woods were said to have been removed during the wars with the native Irish to deny cover to the king's enemies.[46] They fell into Sir George Hodson's possession through the 1839 deed of partition. Some 26 acres were subsequently walled in, incorporated into Hodson's demesne and planted, apparently without controversy. Sir George was a benevolent if paternalistic landlord, a member of the board of guardians and the local dispensary and famine relief committees. He was a provider of local employment. The enclosure took place around the famine year of 1847 and he paid off at least one of the local people. Moreover, the locals would have welcomed wall-building employment.[47] Nevertheless the wall-building copper-fastened Hodson's claim to this addition to his property.

The number of inhabitants within Barchuillia Commons townland dropped by 55 per cent between 1841 and 1851, a much greater loss than the 25 per cent drop in the population of Kilmacanogue parish generally; the number of houses dropped by some 50 per cent in the same decade.[48] Later, the number of squatted-on holdings on Barchuillia Commons fell from 17 to six between 1850 and 1920.[49] This appears to be due to the clearance of houses, to emigration and to the relocating of families, but not to further enclosure. Hodson's near neighbour, Lord Meath of Kilruddery on the eastern flank of the mountain, was said according to local memory around 1910, to have attempted to move the boundary wall of his demesne up to the top of the ridge. Local opinion had thwarted this however, despite his offer to build a chapel in return for public support.[50] A small proportion of the commons was already being cultivated in the 1840s and much turf-cutting had been taking place there.[51]

In 1910, a letter sent to the 'Office of Woods' which administered crown lands, stated that poor people lived in small take-in plots on the commons on the hill, and locals from around Kilmacanogue ran goats, donkeys and sheep on the hillside without knowing what their rights were, or whether they had any. 'They just run them, that's all'. The letter continued:

> one or two more aggressive characters than the others would like to impress the countryside that they are 'owners' and call it 'my hill etc'. It seems that from time to time there have always been very poor people of this class knocking around.

It went on to state:

> small plots [of] a quarter acre or so are constantly enclosed with hill stones by anyone, a one room affair erected on the plot, and the whole sold to someone else for £5 or about, so that plot upon plot has been deliberately taken and sold without a question as to their right to do so, and the documents assigning these plots consist (as I have seen them) of dirty half sheets of notepaper, signed by someone who made a mark 'X' and could not write.[52]

The letter was received in connection with an application from local man and one-time county councillor Arthur Dillon, 'a man of intelligence and education, [who] appears to be of a rather better class than one would expect to find living in a squatter's hut', to purchase or rent from the crown, a plot on the commons. Although a plot was duly assigned, the marking pegs put down by Dillon were removed by people claiming to have grazing rights. An official thought that, rather than visit the site again, it was 'probably more judicious to allow local feeling to die down'. Moreover, legal action was threatened both by Sir George Hodson and by local graziers. Hodson had a prima facie case: having taken possession in 1839, at worst he now held the property as a squatter for over 40 years; this claim might have been countered, however, as the greater part of the commons had never been fenced off by him and was still apparently subject to the interests of commoners such as graziers. Dillon died a few years later without taking up the allotment.[53]

Around Kilmacanogue the landlords enclosed hundreds of acres but not without reaction by the peasantry, some of whom were not themselves so principled as to eschew enclosure on their own account; in Bray, by contrast, after some agitation, a generally-agreed enclosure scheme was achieved.

4. Bray: a structured solution

Bray Commons was an example of a commons which was formally enclosed by act of parliament. It was located on the manor lands originally granted to Walter de Riddlesford around 1173, and its common is specifically referred to as early as 1311. Lord Meath claimed to be 'lord of the soil' as successor-in-title to George Kirk who was granted a patent by Charles I in 1629.[1] The Down Survey showed that the equivalent of 67 statute acres of Bray commons lay at Little Bray within the parish of Old Connaught, Co. Dublin. This probably underestimated the acreage by a quarter to a third; it had been reduced to 57 acres by 1859 when its enclosure was proposed. James McFadden, an objector to the enclosure bill, claimed that the portion being enclosed was 'not one-tenth of the [original] commons'.[2] An eight-acre section of Bray Commons townland, owned by Lord Powerscourt and occupied by a few small-holders and cottiers, lay below Ardmore, within Bray parish and Co. Wicklow, but it was no longer common land in 1859. Moreover, the act specifically limited the 'Upper Commons' to Co. Dublin, leaving Powerscourt unaffected.[3]

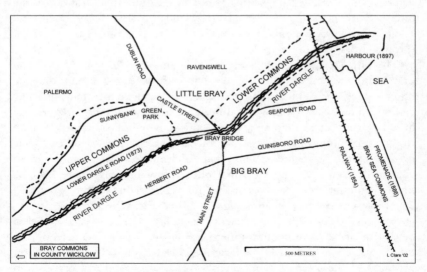

5 Location map – Bray Commons. The Commons, in two sections, is surrounded by the dotted line. The river was the boundary between Counties Dublin and Wicklow.

Neither was the 'sea commons' along the strand south of the river included. This commons was split among two owners: Lord Meath who owned the shore from the Dargle river to the Cockbrook stream, which flowed into the sea opposite the present Strand Hotel, and the Putland family who held from the stream to Bray Head.[4] Lord Meath had more control than Putland over his commons; his houses and cottages were almost all built to a building line inside the embryonic Strand Road. This commons in general remains even now in public use, as Lord Meath leased it to William Dargan who laid it out as a lawn or esplanade, and maintained it during his lifetime, after which the town commissioners took it over in the public interest.[5] The Putland family, or their predecessors, on the other hand, had allowed fisher-folk to build their cottages in an unplanned, disorderly fashion, beside the shore, and George Putland attempted to bring them under control in 1825 by inducing some 20 or so existing cottiers to append their marks in lieu of signatures, on a 99 year 'lease' at 5*d*. each per annum in respect of their 'houses, cabins, lands and gardens'. The 'lease' however was defective and the subsequent rents had not been collected regularly, so that when George's brother Charles inherited the estate and prepared to try to enforce the deed, some fishermen claimed 'adverse possession' or squatters' rights. Despite getting little encouragement from his counsel, Putland ultimately succeeded in regaining acknowledgement of his ownership, but not possession of the fishermen's 'houses, cabins, lands and gardens'.[6] The original unplanned layout of the fishermen's cabins on the Strand Road between the Strand Hotel and the Bray Head Hotel, still compares badly in planning terms with the formal layout of the northern (Lord Meath's) end of the road.[7]

The other traditional rights on the sea commons, drawing of sand and gravel from the beach, removal of sea-rack or sea-weed for manure, drawing up of rowing boats onto the rough marram grass above the high water line and spreading out the fishing nets to dry, led to many disputes between the local population and the entrepreneurs of the new holiday resort. In 1870 the town commissioners lost a case for banning boats from the esplanade because of 'the prescriptive right of the fishermen to have them there'. In 1871, fishermen and supporters met outside town commissioner Breslin's hotel, to protest about 'encroachments on public rights on the sea-shore'. The protesters passed resolutions against 'illegal' enclosure of the sea-shore, encroachments on fishermen's rights, spending of rates 'for the special benefit of one or two commissioners' and neglect of the southern end of the sea-shore where most of the fishermen lived. Eventually a boat-slip was provided by the town commissioners.[8] Removal of sand and gravel from beaches was eventually prohibited by law as an anti-coastal-erosion measure.[9] The sea commons' main claim to fame, for some people, is that in 1773 a property advertisement for nearby Seafield had referred to an adjoining commons 'famous for that manly exercise called goff [golf]'. This is one of

6 '*On the commons of Bray*' – [coloured] Aquatint by Francis Jukes
(1745–1812) (Courtesy of National Library of Ireland)

the earliest references to the game of golf in Ireland.[10] For others its
historical interest relates to the murder on the 'sea commons' of two men
by the Bray Yeomanry in 1798. The actual spot of this incident appears
however to have been north of the river on the 'North Strand' or 'Back
Strand', part of which was included in the enclosure act.[11]

The Bray commons at Little Bray, was composed of two parcels of land,
totalling 57 acres. The lower commons totalling 15 acres lay along the north
bank of the Dargle river below Bray Bridge, where Bray Golf Club was
located prior to its move to Bray Head. The 42-acre upper commons was
located west of the 'town' of Little Bray, and between Sunnybank and the
river.[12] The village of Little Bray was probably formed in the distant past by
traders establishing booths on the commons close to the bridge at the
entrance to the town of Greater Bray. The name Little Bree appears as early
as 1518, while in 1611 Little Bray was defined as being freehold, not part of
the manor of Bray.[13] The commons was a valuable resource for the people
of Bray. It included a network of rights-of-way, an area of poor quality
grazing for cattle, horses, asses, goats, sheep and pigs, as well as poultry and
geese. It was a place for the slaughtering of animals, a source of gravel and
sand for building, a storage space for timber, a place for fishermen to dry
their nets and to land 'sea-rack' or seaweed. Cargo boats were let settle on
the mud, now the site of Ravenswell Road, for unloading. Children played
on the commons, and adults walked with their dogs.[14] Bray Races, with
their ancillary entertainments and hangers-on, were held annually on the
commons with the support of the gentry who, in 1834, enlarged and tidied
up the course and provided a 'stand-house' to accommodate several hundred

spectators. After the course was destroyed by flood in 1839, public sub-scriptions financed employment of 'a large number of persons' to level and improve it once again.[15] In the 1830s, six cattle fairs and four frieze fairs were held each year in Bray. These overflowed from the Main Street, around the old court house and along Castle Street onto the lower commons. Besides the core trading in produce, there were contemporary references to 'show tents', 'show women' and booths selling 'fairings' (small presents) for farmers to bring home to wives and children.[16] The railway along the shore, the new Wicklow mail coach road along Sunnybank, and the Church of Ireland schools at Bray Bridge were all constructed on the commons, the schools on a site granted by Lord Meath in 1819.[17]

Control over the commons had dwindled in the period before enclosure, there previously had been summonses, but 'latterly they do what they like'. Removal of large amounts of sand and gravel despoiled the surface and left some of it under water at times. Squatters nibbled at the edges, erecting make-shift huts, and later permanent dwellings. One section was 'inhabited by a very wretched description of squatter ... when they have built a cabin and made a little bit of garden, they go on taking more year after year'. Some had already acquired, and sold on, their squatters' rights. The squatters appear to have been mainly grouped between Sunnybank and where Greenpark Road was later constructed. It was estimated that four or five acres had been taken in by encroachments, with about 50 squatters in all living on the commons.[18] Nevertheless, there were some attempts to protect the commons. In 1844 the Revd Sir Samuel Hutchinson brought 'several of the respectable inhabitants of the town' before the petty sessions under the acts against skinning and destroying the surface of a commons as a result of their employ-ing a large number of people to level and resurface the course for the holding of the Bray races. He sought a fine of £5 in each case. The first few cases were lost on technicalities but one defendant insisted that the case against him proceed on its merits. Hutchinson's barrister refused to proceed and the charge was dismissed.[19] Hutchinson himself was accused of having enclosed part of the commons around 1840, paying off the occupants of the cabins located there. Nevertheless, there was some resistance, as a new enclosing wall was levelled. Moreover, a map dated 1788 showed 'commons' close to the recent Sunnybank Inn, and adjoining Hutchinson's land at Palermo. This was enclosed before 1838 – if the map was correct.[20] In 1843, Captain Donnellan a large property owner, had taken actions against a roads contractor and others for removing gravel which they were screening close to the river below Bray bridge. The acts against 'skinning' the commons were again used. The cases collapsed on a technicality and Donnellan could only claim by way of consolation that he had 'roused the people of Bray to protect their rights'.[21]

Bray's building boom which followed the arrival of the railway in 1854, triggered a move by some of the landowners to improve the commons. Statutory notice of an Inclosure bill was published in November 1858, but not, as the protesters noted, in the papers which they were accustomed to read.[22] It took three months for word of the proposed enclosure to reach the town of Bray, causing an immediate public outcry. P.W. Jackson, chairman of the town commissioners, who was himself a petitioner for the bill, and, as an adjoining land-owner, a potential beneficiary from the enclosure, called a public meeting to report on the proposals. It was a damage limitation exercise and he undertook to try to delay the passage of the bill pending full consultation.[23] Jackson showed his ability as a consensus politician, when a week later he was called to the chair at a crowded protest meeting in the court house. This gathering had been convened by John Clifton, a vintner of Castle Street. John Critchley, also of Castle Street, a wheelwright and 'a bit of a timber merchant', and Andrew Southern, the mill-owner, were Clifton's most vociferous supporters. This trio collected hundreds of signatures to a petition opposing the bill.[24] Jackson explained that the bill proposed to establish machinery to enclose the land, to sell off part to pay for improvements and expenses, to recognize the title of squatters and others with rights, to build a public path through it and to use the balance to establish a park for the recreation of the inhabitants. This was, perhaps, stretching the truth somewhat; the bill had proposed a public park of only two acres. Most protest was directed at the lack of consultation rather than the principle of tidying up the commons, but the more radical objectors proposed a motion referring to 'confiscation of Bray Commons', 'land-aggrandising parties', 'privileges of our fathers', and 'making the poor poorer and the rich richer'. This motion was refused by Jackson the chairman. A further proposal for the local people to try to manage the commons themselves was not pressed.[25] Perspectives on commons enclosures reflected social class. While the land owners typically regarded the inhabitants as encroachers on property; the people saw the landed gentry as land-grabbers. Jackson closed the meeting, promising again to try to delay the bill pending public discussion, and undertaking to campaign for a much bigger public park; he later claimed on oath that the bill's two-acre park proposal was not of his making and was to have been changed before submission of the bill. He publicly advocated a much larger park. Pledges to prevent the passing of the bill as it stood had been secured by the locals from the two MPs for Co. Dublin, Messrs Taylor and Hamilton.[26]

The bill was passed by the house of lords. While the reports of their select committee hearings on the bill are not generally extant, one aspect considered was whether or not village inhabitants – as opposed to tenants of lands – should have a hearing; eventually it was decided to admit them, that is, any of them who could afford to travel to London![27] When the bill reached the examining committee in the house of commons, its origin was closely probed. Apparently Justice Keogh of Violet Hill initially approached John Ball Greene, a civil engineer of Killiney who later became one of the Bray Commons commissioners, asking him to approach Mr Jackson and

Lord Meath, about the proposal. Greene then went around collecting the signatures of the major land owners as petitioners for the bill: Lord Meath, Lord Powerscourt, Phineas Riall, Colonel Frederick De Butts, Peter Jackson, Sidney Herbert, and others. When asked whether he had consulted the inhabitants, he sniffed 'I preferred collections of opinions of people of position and wealth'. Keogh also approached Peter Sharkey who later became solicitor for the bill, and later still solicitor for the Bray Commons commissioners, a post he resigned after he had represented one of the claimants, Colonel De Butts, before the commissioners. After the bill was published, Lord Meath insisted that it be altered to allocate him the 15-acre lower commons by right of his being lord of the manor, in addition to whatever other allocation would be due on foot of his other interests. The bill had been altered in the earl's favour.[28] Lord Meath wrote from Paris to Phineas Riall, a local landowner and promoter of the bill, claiming that the first he had heard about the detailed content of the bill, was two days before its second reading. He felt that a meeting of those with legal interests in the commons should have been held and a majority view acted on. He anticipated a great clamour from 'encroachers with no rights' but considered it a great advantage to have the 'unsightly waste defaced by dung heaps, carcases and animals' replaced with a road across it, neatly built houses and a public walk along the river.[29]

Other hidden agendas emerged in cross-examination: George Brett, civil engineer, was promised a job as a Commons commissioner but his name was removed in the house of lords on the grounds that two commissioners were sufficient. He gave evidence of learning that Sidney Herbert wanted to enhance his lands in Great Bray as 'villa ground' by transferring his pauper tenants to land he would purchase on the enclosed commons; William Dargan, then developing Quinsboro road, was anxious to have the nuisance of loiterers eliminated from the lower commons across the river; Lord Meath had extracted a considerable price for his consent. To Lord Meath's credit, however, he could, as lord of the manor, have withdrawn the bill but despite some reservations, he refrained from exercising this right.[30]

Certain abuses were criticized during the hearing of evidence. The storage of timber was described as a screen for 'a public necessity close to the town' as well as for all kinds of nuisances; 'ladies of the first respectability going to attend the nearby schools are exposed to all the nuisances'; 'all the labouring classes go down there and it is quite offensive'. Also criticized was the slaughtering of animals, 'horses slaughtered almost every day', as well as public health nuisances generally. And one witness claimed 'I cannot ride through [the commons] in the evening; it is clearly a most disagreeable place'. Matthew O'Reilly Dease had supported the proposals until he learned of Lord Meath's plan to build small cottages on the lower commons, between his (O'Reilly Dease's) residence at Ravenswell and the river. He then opposed it strongly, claiming more than 50 years' adverse possession of the lower commons by himself and his predecessors in title. This reversal of position greatly increased the costs of the proceedings.[31] James Mc Fadden, solicitor for the McMahon estate which was then being processed in the Landed Estates Court, was one of the few objectors heard. With the court's consent, he opposed the bill because it 'was got up for improving Great Bray at the expense of the proprietors of Little Bray' by the transfer of pauper tenants from some of the 120 or so cabins in Great Bray. There was some discussion of the length of leaseholders' property, no doubt jockeying for position in advance of the assessing of rights. Lord Meath's law agent claimed that the lord had passed on no rights of commonage in his leases.[32]

The house of commons made a few important changes in the bill as passed by the lords. The size of the public park was increased from two to ten acres. The period to qualify for full squatters' rights was increased from 10 to 20 years. A graded payment however, could secure title after ten years' occupation. These changes, which adversely affected squatters, followed arguments by the counsel for two objectors who referred to squatting as 'nothing less than a species of robbery'. Lord Meath's initial allocation was reduced from 15 acres to just 3.5 acres.[33] The house of lords generally accepted these changes and the Bray Commons Inclosure act 1859 became law in August 1859. It established the Bray Commons commissioners, naming William Basil Orpen, barrister-at-law, and John Ball Greene, civil engineer, as paid commissioners. They secured powers to extinguish rights of commonage, set out drains, erect fences, build roads, allot lands for recreation of the inhabitants, allot watering places for cattle, provide a market or fair green, allot lands or payments to holders of rights on the commons, and sell surplus land to finance works and expenditure. Any residue would be shared between the successful claimants of rights of commonage. They could waive this right in favour of the townspeople generally.[34]

The commissioners organized hearings in the court house to process the claims to rights on the commons. But prior to that, Lord Meath fought a rearguard action, claiming that the lower commons was in fact the bed of the river and was therefore his by right. There were two channels there, and the argument was whether or not the true river was confined to the southern channel (see cover illustration). Meath's view was controverted by other witnesses, like Alex Cumming, a coal factor and lime storesman, who argued that the lower commons was only under water when there was a high spring tide and a south-east wind. Otherwise the river hugged the southern shore. Robert Seymour of Seapoint, another coal factor, concurred. He had built a bank along the northern side of the river some 25 years previously, and would unload there rather than at his dock 'when the sea would put them on the north side'. Alfred Southern, recalled a main channel along its present southern course, with a northern channel close to Ravenswell, called 'Paddy Marnan's hole', after the man who built a house there. There was good land in between which became an island at full tide, but that was before the removal of the gravel. John Clifton blamed Lord

Meath for flooding the lower commons by removing sand and gravel. 'It had a beautiful fine sod when I first played common [*camáin*] on it, 40 years ago'. The water had run in the north channel only since the gentlemen took away the surface of the commons about 30 years ago. The people followed them and took sand and gravel. And Lord Meath was 'the first that destroyed our "Upper Commons"'. He himself had, despite fear of transportation, poached the salmon which always ran near the south bank. 'beautiful salmon were in the southern channel'. Lord Meath lost the argument.[35]

About 35 persons successfully claimed squatters' rights, some for more than one encroachment, mostly for plots of less than an acre, some holding sublettings. Others, like John Critchley and John Mackey who claimed for wooden huts on the lower commons, lost out. Mackey had bought his 15-year-old hut for £3. 15s. 0d. He and William Lock eventually turned up at the public auction of the property and publicly claimed possession; they were bought off with alternative sites near what is now Greenpark Road. The various claimants gave direct evidence at the enquiry, and called supporting witnesses. John Clifton was called again and again to confirm situations from memory. He was also employed as a caretaker to stop further removal of gravel.[36]

Clifton was the star witness. His family had held land beside the commons for 200 years 'since [we] came here with the soldiers'. He himself remembered back 55 years. The lower commons had a good green sward when he first played there as a child. The fair had been held on the commons before the schools were built there. The commons was never under water until Lord Meath took the surface some 30 years previously; then 'when the people saw the gentlemen take the surface they followed suit'. The commons boundary, the centre of the river, was marked on the centre of the Bridge: 'I have seen a man sitting at one side of the bridge, with only that [commons and county boundary] stone between him and the constable at the other side with a warrant for him and the constable couldn't take him'. He described the seaward extremity of the grassed commons: 'it went up past high-water mark where the two men were shot in 1798'. Charles Douglas worked for the Hutchinson family of Palermo. He described how people were in the habit of coming at night and erecting wooden huts on the commons. The Hutchinsons 'put the people who were in the cabins off by law and gave them some money, £5 a piece'.[37] Clifton lost a claim to four perches which he had held for 27 years, because it was surrounded by heaps of dung rather than by a fence. However, he won a claim for grazing rights having gone there 50 years previously with sheep for his father and asses for himself. From time to time he kept horses, asses and pigs there for 'stretch leg' (exercise) and when suffering from 'trimble' (a staggering disease). Only locals could officially use the commons although tinkers might put in stray asses.[38] John Critchley, whose family had come from Naas, lost his claim to his unfenced ground for storing timber, even though he had been bringing timber there 'before the great storm of 1839'. But he won his claim to grazing rights, because he put horses on the commons to 'shed their timbers' even though they found little to eat. The grazing rights were measured by the 'collop', the grass for one adult cow.[39]

Surplus lots were auctioned as building ground. Squatters on the lower commons were moved to a section of the main commons. Lord Meath, Henry Jackson and other property owners, also bought many of the lots for building.[40] Due to a boom in property values in Bray during the very years 1859–61, when the property was being auctioned off, the income from sales considerably exceeded what might have been anticipated. Auction proceeds after deducting operational expenses were used to pay successful claimants, apart from those squatters or graziers who were allocated specific plots on foot of claims. There remained a considerable sum for public works. These included the laying out of the People's Park, the building of the river wall alongside the park, and the construction of the Lower Dargle Road alongside its other boundary. There remained a gap in both the river wall and the road, because of a wedge of private land between the park and Bray bridge. Although the intervening land owners soon completed the wall, land acquisition difficulties delayed the extension of the Lower Dargle Road, its other boundary.[41]

The commons commissioners provided a platform beside Bray bridge to facilitate the drawing of domestic water by the citizens. They provided three cattle-watering places. They provided space for a fair green, to be developed later by Bray town commissioners. The approved scheme provided for any residue to be divided proportionately between successful claimants unless they waived their rights. An attempt to secure general agreement to donate the balance to the town commissioners was initially successful, but later unravelled, despite a number of statements which had been made at the house of commons enquiry during consideration of the bill that proprietors would give up entitlements for the public good. The Commons commissioners took legal advice which pointed to spending the residue on works for the public benefit, such as developing the recreational open space as a park, and although a final outcome is not on record, from the general context it appears that the greater part of the residue was used up in this way.[42]

The enclosure of Bray Commons was conceived by a cabal of land-owners promoting their own self interests. It was facilitated with little question by the house of lords, but after public outcry it was modified by the house of commons in favour of the inhabitants. It was then implemented professionally without further public dissent. The enclosure brought order to the commons, gave security to long-term squatters, compensated graziers of animals, provided a peoples' park, a river wall, a fair green and other public works. In short, the benefits achieved by the community more than compensated the inhabitants for the loss of their rights of commonage.

Conclusion

Common land and its enclosure represented a temporary pause in the evolution which converted the landmass of these islands from a community resource available to all, into a system of personal ownership of property by powerful individuals. The compromise of commonage which recognised both private property and the shared use of certain lands, emerged from the determined opposition of those who had previously enjoyed the free use of fields and forests. This uneasy compromise broke down in later centuries under further pressure from powerful individuals. It led first to the privatisation of common land deemed surplus to commoners' needs, but later to the complete transition from communal ownership to personal wealth, from social cohesion based on community relationships to a laissez-faire individualism based on personal rights and self-interest, disregarding the rights in equity of those unable to compete politically, legally, economically, or otherwise.

In our detailed case studies, we saw in particular two agencies for enclosure – the landlords and the poverty-stricken squatters, though the investor or speculator was also found lurking in the background. In Dalkey, squatters took over and sold on to speculators. Around Kilmacanogue lands were successfully appropriated by landowners, though not without social agitation; other lands were occupied by squatters. In Bray, after initial dissent, there was a measure of consensus. But the process still goes on.

The analogy between the hovels made with 'a few sticks, furze, fern, etc.' under a dry bank on the roadside commons in Arthur Young's day, and the roadside humpties or tents constructed from a few bent sticks and tarpaulin by the poorest travelling families within our own lifetime, is particularly striking. Moreover, the parallels with past events of newly fenced-in mountain areas, of squatted-on residues from road-widening, of neighbours' attitudes towards groups of travellers, of keep-out signs often in places where previously there was free access, are all too apparent. Ironically, often the most aggressive protection of private property comes from people whose ancestors would have seen themselves as the underdogs. Human nature does not seem to change over the centuries.

Notes

ABBREVIATIONS

CSO/RP	Chief Secretary's Office, Registered Papers	MP	Meath Papers held at Kilruddery, Bray
DEP	*Dublin Evening Post*	NA	National Archives
DHR	*Dublin Historical Record*	NLI	National Library of Ireland
EP	*Evening Packet*	OS	Ordnance Survey
FJ	*Freeman's Journal*	RD	Registry of Deeds
HLRO	House of Lords Record Office	*SN*	*Saunders' Newsletter*
JRSAI	*Journal of the Royal Society of Antiquaries*		

The page numbers in citations of parliamentary papers are the printed page numbers.

The Meath papers were not accessible during the current research; however much material already researched, though not used for the author's previous book, *Victorian Bray*, was utilized.

ACKNOWLEDGEMENTS

1 Peter Pearson, *Between the mountains and the sea* (Dublin, 1998), p. 93.
2 William Brocas (1794–1868), Lower Commons, Bray.

INTRODUCTTION

1 J.H. Andrews, 'The struggle for the public commons' in Patrick O'Flanagan et al. (eds), *Rural Ireland, 1600–1900: modernisation and change* (Cork, 1987), pp 1–23.
2 W.G. Hoskins and L. Dudley Stamp, *The common lands of England and Wales* (London, 1963), pp 1–13, 27; J.M. Neeson, *Commoners, common right, enclosure and social change in England, 1700–1820* (Cambridge, 1993), p. 1; Richard Parry and Barnaby Howes, *The law of easements* (London, 1910), p. 24.
3 H.S. Bennett, *Life on the English manor* (Cambridge, 1948), pp 41–60.
4 Hoskins and Stamp, *Common lands*, p. 4; Neeson, *Commoners*, p. 59ff; E.C.K. Gonner, *Common land and enclosure* (London, 1912), pp 5–16.

5 Gonner, *Common land*, p. 16.
6 Hoskins and Stamp, *Common lands*, pp 81–2; Andrews, 'The struggle for the public commons', p. 1.
7 Hoskins and Stamp, *Common lands,* pp 3–13, 28, 31, 38–43, 4, 8, 221, 65–75, 79–84.
8 F.H.A. Aalen, *Man and the landscape in Ireland* (London, 1978), pp 117–22; J. Otway-Ruthven, 'The organisation of Anglo-Irish agriculture in the middle ages' in *JRSAI*, lxxxi (1951), pp 1–13.
9 Fergus Kelly, *Early Irish farming* (Dublin, 1997), pp 406–8; S.J. Connolly (ed.), *Oxford companion to Irish history* (Oxford, 1998), p. 493; E. Estyn Evans, 'Some survivals of the Irish openfield system' in *Geography*, xxiv (1939), pp 26–8.
10 *Appendix to report of royal commission to enquire into municipal corporations in Ireland*, Part II, [28], HC, 1835, xxviii, p. 928; Part III [26], HC, 1836, xxiv, pp 1005, 1055, 1105ff, 1115ff.
11 Andrews, 'Struggle for the commons', pp 2–5.

1. THE CONTEXT OF ENCLOSURE IN BRITAIN AND IRELAND

1 F.H.A. Aalen, 'The origin of enclosures in eastern Ireland' in Nicholas Stephens and Robin E. Glasscock (eds), *Irish Geographical Studies in honour of E. Estyn Evans* (Belfast, 1970), p. 209; R.A. Butlin, 'The enclosure of open fields and extinction of common rights in England *c.*1600–1750: a review' in H.S.A. Fox and R.A. Butlin, (eds) *Change in the countryside, essays on rural England 1500–1900* (London, 1979), p. 65.
2 Alan Harding, *England in the 13th century* (Cambridge, 1993), pp 93–4, 281; Bennett, *English manor*, pp 57–8; www.met.police.uk./merton/normans.htm, viewed 18 Oct. 2003; *Statute Law Revision Bill and explanatory memorandum 1981*; Henry Berry (ed.), *Statutes and ordnances and acts of parliament of Ireland, King John to Henry V* (Dublin, 1907).
3 Hoskins and Stamp, *Common lands*, pp 50–2.
4 See reference to Statute of Merton above.
5 Gonner, *Common land*, pp 43–69.

6   Hoskins and Stamp, *Common lands*, pp 53–63; J.M. Neeson, *Commoners*, pp 7ff.

7   Hoskins and Stamp, *Common lands*, pp 60–2; J.M. Neeson, *Commoners*, pp 297–9.

8   G.E. Mingay, *The agricultural revolution – changes in agriculture 1650–1880* (London, 1997), pp 63–4.

9   *Dictionary of national biography* (London, 1909), xxi, pp 1272–8; G.E. Mingay, (ed.), *Arthur Young and his times* (London, 1975), p. 12; Arthur Wollaston Hutton (ed.), *Arthur Young's tour in Ireland (1776–9)* (2 vols London, 1897), ii, pp 26, 29.

10 *Encyclopaedia Britannica* (1959 edition) v, pp 899–903; *Political Register*, 14 Apr. 1821, quoted in John Barrell, *The idea of a landscape and a sense of place (1730–1740): an approach to the poetry of John Clare* (Cambridge, 1972), p. 198; Denis Knight (ed.), *Cobbett in Ireland – a warning to England* (London, 1984), pp 19–27.

11 *Encyclopaedia Britannica* (1959 edition), vi, pp 124–7; Hoskins and Stamp, *Common lands*, p. 62.

12 Hoskins and Stamp, *Common lands*, p. 58; David Hey (ed.), *The Oxford companion to local and family history* (Oxford, 1998), pp 151–4.

13 W.H. Minchinton, 'Commissioners of enclosure' in *Essays in Agricultural History*, ii (Newton Abbot, 1968), p. 91.

14 A.W.B. Simpson, *A history of the land law* (Oxford, 1986), p. 261; Hoskins and Stamp, *Common lands*, pp 80–1; R.D. Stewart-Brown, *A guide to compulsory purchase and compensation* (London, 1962), p. 19.

15 John Clare, 'The Mores', in John Barrell and John Bull (eds), *The Penguin book of English pastoral verse* (London, 1982), p. 415, quoted in Neeson, *Commoners*, pp 5–6.

16 Barrell, *Idea of a landscape*, *Appendix, John Clare and the enclosure of Helpston*, pp 189–215.

17 Austin Dobson (ed.), *The poems of Oliver Goldsmith* (London, 1893), pp 27–9.

18 B.J. Graham and L.J. Proudfoot, *An historical geography of Ireland* (London, 1993), pp 74–6; Aalen, 'Origin of enclosures', p. 213.

19 Robert Simington, *The civil survey (1654–1656)*, (10 vols Dublin,

1931–61); Thomas Larcom, *History of the Cromwellian survey of Ireland, 1655–6* (Dublin, 1851), p. 48; Andrews, 'Struggle for the commons', p. 5.

20 *First report of royal commission on municipal corporations*, [23], HC, 1835, xxvii, passim.

21 Ibid., p. 221; Connolly, *Oxford companion*, pp 8–9; Andrews, 'Struggle for the commons', pp 7–8.

22 Aalen, *Man and the landscape*, p. 160.

23 *Appendices E and F to first report of the royal commission on the condition of the poorer classes in Ireland*, [37], HC, 1836, xxxii, passim; [38], HC, 1836, xxxiii, passim.

24 Hutton, *Arthur Young's tour*, pp 95–9.

25 Connolly, *Oxford companion*, p. 5; David Broderick, *The first turnpike roads* (Cork, 2002), pp 86–7; *Irish Builder*, 15 Mar. 1881.

26 K.H. Connell, 'The colonisation of waste land in Ireland, 1780–1845' in *Economic History Review*, iii, no. 1 (1950), p. 45.

27 Connolly, *Oxford companion*, pp 171, 493.

28 Colin Sara, *Boundaries and easements* (London, 1996), p. 139.

29 John Bush, *Hibernia Curiosa* (London, 1769), p. 27.

30 Hutton, *Arthur Young's tour*, pp 39–40.

31 *First report re municipal corporations*, p. 34; *appendix to same*, Parts I ([27], HC, 1835, xxvii/xxviii,), Parts II and III passim, but especially pp 7, 34, 217, 739, 253, 1115, 1116.

32 Ibid., passim.

33 Ibid., passim; NLI, P 12, fiche 51, Thorp collection, pamphlet 729, *The case of John Percival Esquire complaining of a breach of the privileges of the house of commons … 1704*.

34 Ibid., passim.

35 Ibid., passim; *Appendix F to report on poorer classes*, p. 98.

36 Andrews, 'Struggle for the commons', p. 6; Niall McCullough, *Dublin, an urban history* (Dublin, 1989), pp 24–5; www.bansteadcommonsconservat ors.com, viewed 2 Nov. 2003.

37 'New Road' on John Taylor, *Environs of Dublin* (map) (Dublin, 1816). Robert Jennings, *Calary church and parish, Diocese of Glendalough, 150th anniversary pamphlet, 1834–1984* (Calary, 1984), not paginated.

38 13 Geo. II, c. 13, in *The statutes at large passed by the parliaments of Ireland from 1310 to 1791 in 15 volumes (Dublin 1791), (the series extended to 20 volumes by 1800)*, vi, p. 539, *An act for amending and repairing the highway from Belfast to Randallstown to the ferry of Tuam*; *FJ*, 16 Jan. 1843.

39 Aalen, *Man and the landscape*, p. 165; Hervey Mountmorres, *Impartial reflections on the present crisis … [including a general system of enclosures]* (London, 1796), pp 25–6.

40 31 Geo. III, c. 50, (*Irish statutes*, xv, p.807); 40 Geo. III, c. 62 (*Irish statutes*, xx, p. 787).

41 40 Geo. III, c. 97, (*Irish statutes* xx, p. 951).

42 Mountmorres, *Impartial reflections*, pp 25–6. Some enclosure bills had been considered previously, but not passed.

43 Ibid., p. 52.

44 33 Henry VIII, c. 10 (*Irish statutes*, i, p. 186), *An act for jointenant (sic)*.

45 *Statute Law revision bill 1981, explanatory memorandum*, p. 2.

46 9 William III c. 12 (*Irish statutes*, iii, p. 412), *An act for obtaining partitions of lands in coparcenary, joint-tenancy and tenancy in common and bounding and mearing of lands*; 6 Anne, c. 3, (*Irish Statutes*, iv, p. 119), *An act to amend* [the previous act].

47 2 Geo. I, c. 12, (*Irish statutes*, iv, p. 356).

48 8 Geo. I, c. 5, (*Irish statutes*, v, p. 21).

49 Mountmorres, *Reflections*, p. 43.

50 5 Geo. II, c. 9 (*Irish statutes*, v, p. 512).

51 *Fourth report of the commissioners of enquiry into the nature and extent of the bogs in Ireland*, p. 12, (131), 1813/14, vi, Pt II; *Minutes of evidence to the select committee on emigration from the United Kingdom* (237), HC, 1826–7, v., p. 342/3. *Minutes of evidence to the select committee on the condition of the labouring poor in Ireland …* (561), HC, 1823, vi., p. 25.

52 *Cobbett's Parliamentary Debates [of the United Kingdom] (Hansard)*, v, 20 May 1805.

53 Aalen, 'Origin of enclosures', p. 217.

54 NAI, Office of Woods file I 790, legal advice re Lusk commons; *Appendix to report re municipal corporations*, Parts I and II, pp 739, 905.

55 Connolly, *Oxford companion*, p. 171; Andrews, 'Struggle for the commons', pp 9–10.

56 Andrew Lyall, *Land law in Ireland* (Dublin, 2000), pp 449–50; Sunniva McDonagh (ed.), *Irish law Reports [of cases] in the High Court, Court of Criminal Appeal and the Supreme Court,* (Dublin, 1992), i, pp 297–313, re case at Glennamaddoo and Bunnahowna, Co. Mayo; *Annual report of the Irish Land Commission, 1971–2*, (L1–46), pp 6–9.

57 1 & 2 Geo. IV, c. 21, re enclosure of Tallaght, Killsallaghan or Kilsoughlan and Luske, 1821; NAI, Quit Rent Office Records, documents relating to sales of Kilmainham … Kilsallaghan … 1800–34, at 2B–42–144.

58 *The compleat Irish traveller* (London, 1788), i, p. 81.

59 NAI, Official papers, 507/7.

60 Griffiths Valuation, *Ballymore Eustace parish, Co. Kildare.*

61 Thomas Carlyle, *Reminiscences of my Irish journey, 1849* (London, 1882), pp 74–5.

62 Caoimhín Ó Danachair, 'Old houses at Rathnew, Co. Wicklow' in *Béaloideas*, v, (1935), pp 211–2; Stanley J. O'Reilly, 'The Village', in *Ireland's Own*, Apr. 2003, p. 46; *Evidence to the royal commission on the state of law and practice regarding occupation of land in Ireland (Devon Commission)* Part III, p. 705, [657], 1845, xxi.

63 *Census of Population Co. Wicklow, 1851.*

64 29 Geo. III, c. 30 (*Irish statutes*, xiv, p. 1102).

65 31 Geo. III, c. 38 (*Irish statutes*, xv, p. 763).

66 36 Geo. III, c. 50 (*Irish statutes*, xvii, p. 1129); Andrews, 'Struggle for the commons', p. 23 (footnote 43); *Appendix to report re municipal corporations*, Part I, p. 780.

67 Walter Fitzgerald, 'The Curragh – its history and traditions', in *Journal of the Co. Kildare Archaeological Society*, iii, No. 1, (1889), pp 1–16.

68 *Griffith's Valuation Rathmichael parish, Co. Dublin; FJ*, 18 Aug. 1847; 29 Geo. III, c. 30; see Ballymore Eustace Registration case below.

69 *Report and minutes of select committee on the enclosure and regulation of commons* (85) HC, 1913, vi; (Question 464), p. 43.

70 Preamble to 31 Geo. III, c. 38 (*Irish statutes*, xv, p. 763); *Appendix to first report re municipal corporations*,

Part I, p. 173; OS namebooks, Co. Wicklow, pp 321–2.

71 *Minutes of evidence to select committee on the disturbed state of Ireland*, p. 103 (677), 1831/2, xvi; NA '320–327', 2B–44–3, Quit Rent Office papers, case on behalf of George Culley, p. 6.

72 *Minutes re disturbed state of Ireland*, p. 103.

73 Case on behalf of George Culley, p. 8; *Mins of evidence to select committee into state of Ireland with references to disturbances* (129), HC, 1825, viii. p. 438.

74 *Appendix E to report on poorer classes*, p. 43.

75 2 & 3, Will. IV, c. 88.

76 *Evidence re state of Ireland with references to disturbances*, p. 438.

77 John C. Alcock, *Registry cases 1832–1837* (Dublin, 1837), pp 36–41 (Microfilm NLI, POS 7428).

78 John Barrell, *Idea of landscape*, p. 207.

79 Extracted from list of townlands in *Griffith's Valuation, Co. Dublin*.

80 M.J. McEnery and Raymond Refaussé, *Christ Church deeds* (Dublin, 2001), deeds nos 386, 1635; NLI, Ms 100, Materials for the history of county Dublin including extracts of original documents c.1200–1800; James Mills (ed.), *Account roll of the Holy Trinity, Dublin, 1337–1346* (Dublin, 1996 edition), p. 174.

81 Aalen, 'Origin of enclosures', pp 213–21.

82 Raymond Gillespie, 'The archbishops of Dublin and their estate maps' in Raymond Refaussé and Mary Clark (eds), *A catalogue of the maps of the estates of the Archbishops of Dublin* (Dublin, 2000), pp 22–4.

83 McEnery and Refaussé *Christ Church deeds*, deeds nos. 1490, 1189, 1691.

84 Raymond Gillespie, 'Small worlds: settlement and society in the royal manors of sixteenth century Dublin' in H.B. Clarke and Jacinta Prunty (eds), *Surveying Ireland's past: multi-disciplinary essays in honour of Anngret Simms*, (Dublin, 2004), pp 197–216.

85 Anngret Simms, 'Newcastle as a medieval settlement' in *Newcastle Lyons – a parish in the Pale* (Dublin, 1986), p. 22.

86 Edmund Curtis, (ed.), 'The court book of Esker and Crumlin' in *JRSAI*, lix (1929), p. 139.

87 Ibid. pp 137–144; Curtis, 'Court Book' in *JRSAI*, lx (1930), p. 40.

88 Finola Watchorn, *Crumlin, the way it was* (Dublin, 1985), pp 30–3.

89 John D'Alton, *The history of Co. Dublin* (reprint Cork, 1976), p. 349.

90 *Journal of the Irish house of commons, 1735 and 1751*; 58 Geo. III, c. 28, re enclosure of Kilmainham, St James, Clondalkin, Crumlin, Newcastle and Rathcoole, 1818; Watchorn, *Crumlin*, pp 30–3.

91 Curtis, 'Court book', p.133.

92 Gillespie, 'Small worlds'.

93 H.B. Clarke, *Irish Historic Towns Atlas No. 11, Dublin, Part I, to 1610* (Dublin, 2002), p. 24; J.T. and R.M. Gilbert (eds), *Calendar of ancient records of Dublin* (1899–1944), ii, 116, 120.

94 P.J. Stephenson, 'The green area of St. Stephen' in *DHR*, vii, no. 1, (Dec. 1944–Sept. 1945), pp 92–102.

95 McCullough, *Urban history*, pp 24–5, 39.

96 Francis Elrington Ball *A history of the County Dublin* (reprint Dublin, 1979), vi, p. 108; William Cotter Stubbs, 'Finglas Co. Dublin vestry books' in *JRSAI*, xlvi, Part I (1916), page 36; Michael Tutty, 'Finglas' in *DHR*, xxvi (Dec. 1972 – Sept. 1973) pp 66–73.

97 For example, two at Kilmainham – Seosamh Ó Broin, *Inchicore, Kilmainham and district* (Dublin, 1999), p. 31; Harold's Cross Green, Joe Curtis, *Harold's Cross* (Dublin, 1998), p. 1.

98 Joseph Archer, *Statistical survey of the County of Dublin* (Dublin, 1801), pp 215–19.

99 Aalen, 'Origin of enclosures', p. 221.

100 Peadar Bates, *Donabate and Portrane, a history* (n.p., 1988), p. 195.

101 NLI, Microfilm P712. Notice re petition for commons inclosure bill, British Library additional manuscript, 40,260, f. 319.

102 1 & 2 Geo. IV, c. 21.

103 *Griffith's Valuation* compared with OS sheets; Aalen, 'Origin of enclosures', p. 221.

104 *FJ*, 14 Jul. 1824; NA, State of Country papers 2504–10, 2604–5.

105 NA, CSO/RP, 1824/9037.

DALKEY: SQUATTERS SELL
ON TO SPECULATORS

1   NA, 2B–46–35, Quit Rent Office
    papers, file I 867, Dalkey
    Commons Co. Dublin, report
    from QRO to Commissioners of
    Woods etc., 20 Apr. 1841.
2   Thomas Reading, A map of the
    lands of Dalkey (Sept. 1765), (NLI,
    Map 16–G– 52(5).
3   Charles V. Smith, Dalkey, society and
    economy in a small medieval Irish
    town (Dublin, 1996), p 37.
4   Reading, Dalkey map; Smith,
    Dalkey, p. 38.
5   Weston St John Joyce, The
    neighbourhood of Dublin (Dublin,
    1976 reprint), pp 68, 72–3, 88.
6   J.J. Gaskin, Irish varieties (Dalkey,
    1987 edition), pp 66–7; C.
    Scantlebury, 'A tale of two islands'
    in DHR, 15 (1958), p. 122.
7   NA, 2B–46–35, Quit Rent Office
    papers, report, 20 Apr. 1841;
    Gaskin, Varieties, pp 15, 66; Ball,
    County Dublin i, p.77; FJ, 21 Oct.
    1885.
8   FJ, 21 Oct. 1885.
9   Irish Penny Journal, i, no. 21, 21
    Nov. 1840, pp. 162–3.
10 Gaskin, Varieties, p. 57.
11 Irish Penny Journal, 21 Nov. 1840,
    p. 162.
12 Scantlebury, 'Two islands',
    pp 125–6.
13 NA, OPW/1/8/6/3, p. 127,
    Memorial of Richard Toutcher to
    Kingstown Harbour
    Commissioners, 13 Nov. 1823 and
    p. 154 cross-examination, 8 Jan.
    1824; NLI, Ms 217, Consent for
    materials at Dalkey.
14 Peter Pearson, Dun Laoghaire,
    Kingstown (Dublin, 1981),
    pp 24–6.
15 NA, CSO/RP, 9008/1824.
16 FJ, 23 Oct. 1885.
17 Analysis of Griffith's Valuation for
    Dalkey Commons, pp 20–6,
    (particularly Reference 82) and its
    comparison with information
    contained in various registered
    deeds, various directories, and the
    published works cited elsewhere
    in these notes.
18 F. M. O'Flanagan, 'Glimpses of
    Old Dalkey', in DHR, iv, no. 2
    (Dec. 1941/Feb. 1942), pp 47–8;
    Nicholas Donnelly, Short histories
    of Dublin parishes (Carraig
    chapbooks reprint, n.d.), Part iv,

p. 158; 'The Catholic directory, for
    1821' quoted in Reportorium
    Novum, ii, no. 2 (1960), p. 339;
    Samuel Lewis, A history and
    topography of County Dublin, 1837
    (Cork, 1980 reprint), p.42;
    Griffith's Valuation, parish of
    Dalkey, Co. Dublin, 1848;
    Franciscan library, Killiney, record
    card.
19 Griffith's Valuation, parish of
    Dalkey, Co. Dublin, 1848.
20 For Carey: Griffith's Valuation for
    Dalkey commons, (7 interests) and
    RD,1836–5–147 and others; for
    Parkinson: Griffith's Valuation for
    Dalkey commons and RD,
    1836–18–49 and others; for
    Foster: RD, 1840–20–25 and
    others.
21 For Byrne: Gaskin, Varieties, pp
    99–104; RD, 1836–15–36 and
    others; Thom's Directory, 1853,
    pp 973, 975; for Tyrrell: Griffiths
    Valuation for Dalkey commons;
    he held 11 plots, mainly building
    plots, in fee, and 18 references,
    mainly houses, as immediate
    lessor; Thom's Directory, 1853,
    pp 974, 1189.
22 Thom's Directory, 1861, p. 1391;
    NA, CSO/RP, 1834/9008.
23 OS Co. Dublin 6" Sheet, 23, 1843
    edition.
24 O'Flanagan, 'Glimpses of Old
    Dalkey', pp 43–5.
25 J.C. W. Wylie, Irish Land Law
    (Dublin, 1986), p. 935; William
    Hutch, Mrs Ball – a biography
    (Dublin, 1879), pp 249–50;
    Desmond Forristal, The first Loreto
    sister (Dublin, 1994), pp 106–9;
    O'Flanagan, 'Glimpses of old
    Dalkey', p. 44.
26 FJ, 9 Oct. 1885.
27 RD, 856–437–571938, 1 Sept.
    1829; RD, 856–436–571937, 21
    Sept. 1929; RD, 854–366–570877,
    28 Nov. 1829.
28 FJ, 21 Oct. 1885.
29 Thom's Directory, 1860, p. 1347.
30 NA, QRO files, Office of woods
    file I 867.
31 RD, 1836–15–137; RD,
    1836–15–14; RD, 1836–16–77;
    RD, 1836–16–285; RD,
    1836–19–108; O'Flanagan,
    'Glimpses of Dalkey', pp 45–8.
32 NA, QRO file I 867, letter 30 Jul.
    1850, Jordan Darrah to Sir George
    Grey; NA, LEC, 105/33 Lands of
    Killiney Castle and Obelisk Hill;
    NLI, Map 16–G–41(2) (two
    different maps have the same

number); Peter Pearson, Between
    the mountains and the sea (Dublin,
    1998), p. 60.
33 The oft-quoted suggestion in
    Gaskin, Varieties, pp 97–105, that
    an abortive gold rush fuelled the
    speculation, needs to be
    questioned – but both Pat Byrne
    and Etty Scott's father sold out
    their plots for sites for expensive
    residences!
34 M.R.L. Kelly, Dalkey county Dublin
    (Ilfracombe,1952), pp 31–3; NA,
    LEC 95/11, re Kybher Pass.
35 FJ, 21 Oct. 1885.
36 FJ, 21 Oct. 1885, 19 Oct. 1885;
    Gaskin, Varieties, pp 105–6; FJ, 3
    Nov. 1885; Pearson, Mountains and
    sea, p. 109; FJ, 4 June 1889.
37 Gaskin, Varieties, p. 64; Smith,
    Dalkey, pp 48–50.
38 O'Flanagan, 'Glimpses of Dalkey',
    p. 45; Gaskin, Varieties, p. 18;
    Minutes, Dalkey town
    commissioners, 7 Apr. 1864.
39 Dalkey town commissioners,
    Minutes, 7 Dec. 1885, 13 Jan. 1886.
40 O'Flanagan, Glimpses of Dalkey,
    p. 44; FJ, 9 Oct. 1885.
41 FJ, 19 Oct. 1885 and following
    days.
42 FJ, 9 Oct. 1885 and following
    dates; O'Flanagan, 'Glimpses of
    Dalkey', p. 44.
43 Ibid.
44 FJ, 27 Oct. 1885.
45 NA, CSO/RP 19887, 1885, Police
    reports of meeting.
46 FJ, 3 Nov. 1885; FJ, 3 Dec. 1885;
    Dun Laoghaire/Rathdown county
    council, parks and landscape
    services, leaflet, Sorrento Park
    1884–1984.

2. THE SUGAR LOAVES: SEIZURES BY
SQUIRES SPARK OFF SEDITION

1   Bray People, 8 Oct. 1993.
2   NA, Quit Rent office papers, file I
    920; NLI, PC 8897–8900, Box 12,
    Powerscourt papers, Agreement
    with map, 3 Dec. 1839; RD,
    1839–22–180.
3   Court case below refers to
    'Killough commons'.
4   Hutton, Arthur Young's tour,
    pp 94–104.
5   The compleat Irish traveller, i, p. 44.
6   Robert Frazer, Statistical Survey of
    County Wicklow (Dublin, 1801),
    p. 49.
7   Ibid., p. 56.
8   SN, 25 July 1839.

9 Hutton, *Arthur Young's tour*, ii, pp 47–9.
10 Frazer, *Survey*, p. 244.
11 T. Jones Hughes, 'East Leinster in the mid-nineteenth century' in *Irish Geography*, iii (1958), pp 235–7.
12 *Census of Ireland*, 1841.
13 Henry David Inglis 'A journey through Ireland during the spring, summer and autumn of 1834' in Michael Hurst (ed.), *Contemporary observations of Ireland from Grattan to Griffith* (Bristol, 2000), ii, 16.
14 Mr and Mrs Hall, *Handbooks for Ireland – Dublin and Wicklow* (London, 1853), p. 119.
15 NA., Valuation office field books, O.L. 4.1965, Calary parish, Co. Wicklow.
16 Jennings, *Calary Church and Parish*.
17 Hughes, 'East Leinster', pp 233–4; Rev A.E. Stokes, *The parish of Powerscourt* (Bray 1986), pp 11–12; Kevin Whelan, 'The Catholic parish, the Catholic chapel and village development in Ireland', in *Irish Geography*, xvi (1983), pp 5–6.
18 Ruan O'Donnell, *The rebellion in Wicklow, 1798* (Dublin, 1998), pp 77–80, 184–92; Myles V. Ronan, (ed.), *Insurgent Wicklow, 1798, by Luke Cullen* (Dublin, 1948).
19 *FJ*, 11 July 1832.
20 NA, Outrage papers Co. Wicklow, 1838 (various), 1839 32/10175, 32/7993.
21 *DEP*, 29 Sept. 1846.
22 Ibid.
23 NLI, M 28849 (1), Letters Powerscourt to Sandys, 17 Nov. 1837, 24 Mar. 1838, 10 Dec. 1838, 12 Nov. 1839.
24 NLI, PC 8897–8900, Box 12, Powerscourt papers, Agreement with map, 3 Dec. 1839.
25 NLI, M 28849 (1), Circular, 21 Dec. 1839.
26 NLI, M 28849 (1), Letter, Powerscourt to Sandys, 2 Mar. 1840.
27 NA, CSO/RP 15023/1840 – filed with Outrage papers at 3–703 box-1007, file of correspondence June–Aug. 1840, (Letters, 1 June 1840 and 3 June 1840, Sandys to Dublin Castle).
28 Ibid. (Statement, M. Booth and others, 2 June 1840).
29 Ibid. (Police memo, 2 June 1840).
30 NA, Outrage papers Co. Wicklow, 1838 (various), 1839

32/10175, 32/7993, (Report Lynar, 8 June 1840), Liam Price, 'Powerscourt and the territory of Fercullen', in *JRSAI*, lxxxiii (1953), pp 117–120; Margaret C. Griffith, (ed.), *Calendar of inquisitions, county Dublin* (Irish Record Commission, Dublin, 1991), p. 325.
31 Ibid. (Report Lynar, 8 June 1840); *EP*, 9 June 1840; *FJ*, 16 June 1840.
32 *EP*, 11 and 14 July 1840; *FJ*, 11 July 1840; Hoskins and Stamp, *common lands*, p. 52; *Appendix F* to *Report on poorer classes*, p. 93; *SN*, 11 July 1840.
33 *FJ*, 13 July 1840.
34 NA, CSO/RP 10523/1840, (Police reports, 25 and 30 July 1840).
35 Ibid. (Police reports, 30 July and 7 Aug. 1840).
36 *EP*, 5 Sept. 1840.
37 CSO/RP 15023/1840, (Letters, Sandys to Dublin Castle, 28 July 1840 and 14 Aug. 1840). Kilmacanogue chapel is indeed on a corner of Glencap Commons.
38 *EP*, 5 Sept. 1840.
39 *EP*, 9 June and 14 July 1840; *FJ*, 8 and 14 Sept. 1840.
40 NLI, M 28849 (1), Letters Powerscourt to Sandys, 24 June 1840, 23 July 1840, 8 Oct. 1840, one undated (but datable as 12 June 1840 approx. from local and national references).
41 NLI, M 28849 (1), Circular, 31 Mar. 1841.
42 NLI, M 28849 (1), Undated letter, Powerscourt to Sandys; *FJ*, 24 July 1841; *FJ*, 29 Apr. 1842; *EP*, 30 Apr. 1842; *EP*, 7 July 1842.
43 Charles Mosley (ed.-in-chief), *Burke's peerage and baronetage* (Crans, Switzerland, 1999 edition), ii, p. 2298; *FJ*, 13 Jan. 1845; *FJ*, 15 Dec. 1845; *FJ*, 24 Dec. 1845; *FJ*, 31 Dec. 1845; *EP*, 10 Jan. 1846; *FJ*, 14 Jan. 1846; *FJ*, 16 May 1846, (2 articles); *DEP*, 16 May 1846, (2 articles); *EP*, 19 May 1846; *DEP*, 11 July 1846; *FJ*, 26 Sept. 1846; *DEP*, 19 Sept. 1846.
44 *FJ*, 26 Oct. 1837; *FJ*, 15 Dec. 1845; *FJ*, 24 Dec. 1845; *FJ*, 31 Dec. 1845; *FJ* 14 Jan. 1846; *FJ*, 16 May 1846.
45 *Griffith's Valuation*, Kilmacanogue parish Co. Wicklow, 1851.
46 NA, 2B–46–39, Quit Rent Office papers, file I 920.

47 Comparison between *OS Co. Wicklow, 6" sheet 8*, 1838 and 1937 editions; NA, Quit Rent Office papers, file I 920; NLI, Hodson papers, Mss 16418, p. 23 and 16392, p. 102; Eva O Cathaoir 'The Hodson/Adair family of Hollybrook' in *Journal of the Greystones Archaeological and Historical Society*, ii (2000), pp 58–9; *DEP* 29 Sept. 1846.
48 Census of Ireland 1851.
49 Comparison of *Griffith's Valuation*, Kilmacanogue parish, Co. Wicklow, 1851 with Valuation Office cancelled books *c*.1920.
50 NA, Quit Rent Office papers, file I 920.
51 NA, Valuation Office field books O.L. 1967, Kilmacanogue parish.
52 NA, Quit Rent Office papers, file I 920.
53 Ibid.

4. BRAY: A STRUCTURED SOLUTION

1 K.M. Davies, *Irish historical towns atlas, no. 11, Bray* (Dublin, 1998), pp 1, 11; HLRO, Vol. 7/1859/B5, House of Commons Select Committee on the Bray Commons bill, manuscript notes of proceedings, 21 & 22 July 1859; MP, Box 2, B/19/44/1, Minutes of proceedings, Bray Commons commissioners, 6 Dec. 1859.
2 NLI M. 714, (Microfilm P. 7362), Down Survey parish maps with terriers, of Co. Dublin, copied by Daniel O'Brien in 1786/7; NAI Quit Rent Office file 790 (Lusk) re calculation; Preamble to *Bray Commons Inclosure Act, 1859*, (22 & 23 Vict., cap 75.); *Census of Ireland, General alphabetical index to the townlands and towns, parishes and boundaries of Ireland* (Dublin, 1851), (1992 reprint), p.168; ; HLRO, Vol 7/1859/B5, House of Commons Select Committee on the Bray Commons bill, manuscript notes of proceedings, 21 and 22 July 1859.
3 *OS Co. Wicklow, Sheet 4*, 1838 edition; *Griffith's Valuation*, Bray parish, Co. Wicklow, 1851
4 NLI, Map 16–J–7(2), Alex. Nimmo, Map of shore of Bray showing proposed piers, [c. 1825].
5 Liam Clare, *Victorian Bray, a town adapts to changing times* (Dublin, 1998), p. 37.
6 Copy document dated 23 Mar., 1825, and associated legal advice

held by author; Valuation Office 'cancelled book', Co. Wicklow, Bray no 2 E.D., Townland of Newcourt, *c.* 1880.

7   Clare, *Victorian Bray*, pp 52.
8   Ibid. pp 50–1.
9   *FJ*, 10 Oct., 1884; *FJ*, 22 Sept. 1884; *Royal Commission on coastal erosion, reclamation of tidal lands and afforestation in the United Kingdom, minutes of evidence to third and final report*, Vol III, Part II, [cd 5709], HC, 1911, xiv, p. 176, pars 29866–85.
10   *SN*, 3 May 1773, quoted in William H Gibson, *Early Irish golf* (Naas, 1988), p. 9.
11   Ronan, *Insurgent Wicklow*, pp 13–15; MP, Box 2 B/19/44/1 Bill of evidence for 7 Nov. 1863, quoting proceedings of commission 28 Dec. 1859, pp 48–9 (relating to commons within Co. Dublin only).
12   *Preamble, Bray Commons Inclosure Act, 1859; Dublin Builder*, 1 Sept. 1859.
13   Davies, *Bray Atlas*, p. 8.
14   Numerous references in HLRO Vol 7/1859/B5, House of Commons select committee notes, and in MP, Box 2, B19/44/1, Bill of evidence, 7 Nov. 1863, quoting proceedings of commission 28 Dec. 1859.
15   *FJ*, 18 Sept. 1832 (two articles), *FJ*, 24 Mar. 1834, *FJ*, 18 June 1834, *FJ*, 14 Aug. 1839, *FJ*, 28 Aug. 1844; D'Alton, *County Dublin*, p. 453.
16   *FJ*, 28 Aug. 1844; *FJ*, 30 Sept. 1844; *FJ*, 15 Dec. 1860; *Thom's Directory*, 1847; Bill of evidence, 7 Nov. 1863, pp 40–41, 47; 'An Old Inhabitant' (F J. Symour), *100 years of Bray and its neighbourhood 1770–1870* (Dublin, 1907), p. 35.
17   Davies, *Bray Atlas*, p. 13
18   HLRO, Commons select committee notes, 21 and 22 July 1859; *FJ*, 16 Jan. 1843; *OS Co. Dublin, 25" sheet 26 xiv*, 1867.
19   *FJ*, 28 Aug. 1844.
20   MP, Box 2, B/19/44/1, Minutes Bray Commons commissioners, 2 Jan. 1860; NAI, M6013, Samuel Byron, Map of 'part of the lands of Little Bray' (1788).
21   *FJ*, 16 Jan. 1843.
22   *Dublin Gazette*, 23 Nov. 1858; *FJ*, 25 Feb. 1859.
23   *FJ*, 25 Feb. 1859; *SN*, 25 Feb. 1859.
24   *FJ*, 25 Feb. 1859; *SN*, 25 Feb. 1859; HLRO, Vol 6/1859, House of Lords select committee, minutes of evidence, Bray Commons Inclosure bill, 31 Mar. 1859, p. 92.
25   *FJ*, 25 Feb. 1859; *SN*, 25 Feb. 1859.
26   *FJ*, 25 Feb. 1859; *SN*, 25 Feb. 1859; HLRO, Vol 6/1859, House of Lords select committee, minutes, pp 1–32.
27   *FJ*, 1 Apr. 1859.
28   Journal of the House of Lords, 1859, p. 172, 8 Apr. 1859; HLRO, House of Commons select committee notes, 21 and 22 July 1859.
29   NLI, PC 260 and 261, File 78, Riall papers, undated letter, Lord Meath to 'Riall'.
30   Ibid. and letter 8 Aug. 1859, P.W. Jackson to Riall.
31   Ibid. HLRO, House of Commons select committee notes, 21, 22 and 31 July 1859; NLI, PC 260 and 261 Riall papers, letter 9 Aug. 1959 Jackson to Riall.
32   HLRO, House of Commons select committee notes, 21 and 22 July 1859.
33   Ibid., *FJ*, 27 July 1859.
34   *Bray Commons Inclosure Act, 1859.*
35   *FJ*, 22 Nov. 1859; MP, Box 2, B19/44/1, Bill of evidence, 7 Nov. 1863, p. 34 et seq.
36   MP, Box 2, B19/44/1, Minutes of proceedings, Bray Commons commissioners, 1859–1861; Bill of evidence, 7 Nov. 1863, p. 46 et seq.
37   Ibid. pp 46 et seq., 60 et seq.
38   Ibid., pp 68, 72–3; MP, Box 2, B19/44/1, Minutes of proceedings, Bray Commons commissioners, 1859–1861; MP, Box 2, B19/44/1, Draft award of Bray Commons commissioners 1867, Schedule 4.
39   MP, Box 2, B19/44/1, Bill of evidence, 7 Nov. 1863, pp 65–7, 76; for explanation of 'collop' see *evidence to Devon commission*, I, p. 73.
40   MP, Box 2, B19/44/1, Minutes of proceedings, Bray Commons commissioners, 1859–1861; MP, Box 2, B19/44/1, Draft award of Bray Commons commissioners 1867, Schedule 2.
41   MP, J/2/11, (2), Case on behalf of William B Orpen and John Ball Greene, no date; Bill for earl of Meath for the landed estates court, 20 July 1863; Clare, *Victorian Bray*, pp 33–4, 44–5, 16–17.
42   Clare, *Victorian Bray*, pp 55, 48–9; MP, J/2/11,(2), Case on behalf of William B. Orpen and John Ball Greene, no date; House of Commons Select Committee on the Bray Commons Bill, manuscript notes of proceedings, 21, 22 and 31 July 1859.